Basic Vocabulary Builder

Eugene Ehrlich   Daniel Murphy

McGraw-Hill Book Company

New York • St. Louis • San Francisco • Auckland • Düsseldorf • Johannesburg
Kuala Lumpur • London • Mexico • Montreal • New Delhi • Panama • Paris
São Paulo • Singapore • Sydney • Tokyo • Toronto

10 11 12 13 14 15 FGRFGR 8 9 8 7 6 5

Library of Congress Cataloging in Publication Data

Ehrlich, Eugene H
  Basic vocabulary builder.

  (McGraw-Hill paperbacks)
  1. English language—Dictionaries. I. Murphy,
Daniel Joseph, 1921–   joint author. II. Title.
PE1680.E38   423′.1   75-23328
ISBN: 0-07-019105-0

Preface

The words we need for writing are not necessarily the longest words, the most scholarly words. The words we need for writing are the words that say exactly what we intend to say.

In the past few years, the authors have collected many words that were used mistakenly in their college English classes. These words were then presented to other classes in order to make the final selections of words that most college students would find useful. Thus, while it may seem strange to include relatively common words along with rarely used words, the explanation is that many students in American colleges do not know how to use them.

We sincerely hope this volume will be helpful to students who wish to improve their vocabulary.

Eugene Ehrlich
Daniel Murphy

Contents

Building Your Vocabulary

You will best build your vocabulary by employing a three-part approach:

- systematic exposure to new words through reading
- use of the dictionary to gain understanding of each new word you meet
- regular practice in use of the words

The book you now are reading is designed to supply you with a collection of words arranged in dictionary format. It will teach you a new dictionary habit that will help you get started on a personal program of vocabulary building. When you finish studying this book, you will be able to organize your own efforts in order to master every word you want to learn.

For each word entry in this book, you are supplied with the following:

- syllabication
- pronunciation
- meaning

- derivation
- sample sentences employing the word
- words related to the word entry

Except for the sample sentences, the information is the same as that supplied by a standard dictionary. If you pay attention to each one of these elements, the hours you spend with this book will pay off in an enriched vocabulary and a method for learning the words you meet in your own reading.

The way a word is broken into syllables will guide you in hyphenating words at the ends of lines in your writing. Syllabication will also help you learn the correct spelling of words.

Pronunciation is important, of course, in using words in speech. The pronunciation key that precedes the vocabulary portion of this book tells you how to use the marks that appear above the vowels in the pronunciation entries. The pronunciation used in this book is standard United States pronunciation. Before beginning to work through the book, take the time to acquaint yourself with this key. You may have to consult the key many times before you master it fully.

The definitions that are supplied in this book are the most common definitions of the words. If you feel that you want a more comprehensive grasp of a particular entry, consult any of the standard dictionaries or an unabridged dictionary. Three of the best standard dictionaries are *Webster's Collegiate Dictionary, The American College Dictionary,* and *American Heritage Dictionary.* Some words have so many meanings, however, that not even an unabridged dictionary will list them all.

Word derivations are always interesting and can be useful in learning new words. By the time you have finished your work in this book, you will have become familiar with many of the root words used in English as well as with many common prefixes and suffixes. A list of common prefixes and suffixes is supplied at the end of this book. You must not rely on derivations to give you the meanings of words, but they may supply you with valuable clues.

Sample sentences are supplied for each word entry in order to give you some idea of how words are used. In certain cases, in addition to the word entry itself, the sample sentences employ words related to the principal word entry. For this reason, you must always be alert to the related words supplied in each entry.

As you work through this book, employ the following procedure. Begin with the first word, *allusion*. Do you know what it means? It is a noun, as you can see from the symbol *n.*, which follows its syllabication. If you know what it means, examine its pronunciation to be sure you can pronounce it, and read its meaning to check your understanding. Then read the derivation and the sample sentences. Finally read the related words to make sure you know all of them.

If you do not know the meaning of *allusion* or its related words, employ the following procedure.

Read through the complete entry, including pronunciation, derivation, sample sentences, and related words, as well as meaning. Then turn aside from the book and try to recite the meaning and the sample sentences from memory. If you can do so, put a check mark in the margin next to that word. If you cannot, read the entire entry again and try to recite from memory. When you can, put a check mark in the margin next to the entry. This check mark signifies your first step toward learning the word.

Do not try to complete the book in a single marathon session. Work as long as you can without becoming fatigued. A half an hour is good enough for each session. If you work every day for half an hour, you will be building your vocabulary rapidly.

When you return to your vocabulary work on the second day and on succeeding days, go back over the words you have studied. By just looking at a word, can you recite its meaning from memory? If you can, put a check mark in the margin. If you cannot, study the word again and then recite its meaning. Put a check mark in the margin whenever you can recite the meaning of a word. As the check marks accumulate, the words will become fixed more and more firmly in your memory.

Now you must begin to use in writing the words you have mastered. Caution: use the words only when they are appropriate. Nothing is gained from inventing thoughts to match words you have learned.

You must also expand your reading to include books that challenge your vocabulary. In this way you will have the opportunity to reinforce your memory of the words you have learned, and you will be exposed to more and more new words.

As you encounter new words in your reading, develop your own file of words. Index cards are a handy tool for learning new words. On each card, write the word as the dictionary spells it and syllabicates it. Below the word, write its pronunciation, using the key supplied in this book or using a dictionary pronunciation key. On the back of the card, write two sample sentences that employ the word you want to learn. One of the sentences can be the one from your reading in which the word appears. The other can be one of your own devising.

In this way, you will begin to develop a personal file of words that you can use in the same way that you will use this book. Put a check mark on the card each time you are able to recite the meaning of a word from memory.

The challenge is yours. Good luck.

Pronunciation Key

The following symbols are used to assist you in pronouncing the vocabulary entries in this book:

ā as in hate
ă as in cat
ä as in far
ē as in see
ĕ as in set
ē̃ as in her
ī as in ice
ĭ as in him
ō as in no

ŏ as in hot
ô as in born
oī as in join
ōo as in soothe
ou as in loud
ū as in use
ŭ as in cut
û as in burn

The symbol ′ is used to indicate the syllable of a word on which the primary accent falls. Thus, for example, the word *dictionary* would be written this way: dĭk′shŭn-ĕ-rē.

a **A** a

al-lu-sion *n.* *Pronunciation:* ăl-lōō′zhŭn

Meaning: a reference by indirection or implication, a hint

Derivation: Latin *alludere,* to play with

Examples:

The obscure allusion on page 30 was clarified by a statement on the following page.

She opened her remarks by alluding to the previous speaker, who had made the same point she wished to emphasize.

allude *v.i.*

al-tru-is-tic *adj.*   *Pronunciation:* ăl-tru̅-ĭs′tĭc
  Meaning: devoted to the good of others
  Derivation: French *altruisme*
  Examples:
      Nora wished to save her altruistic impulses for
      causes worthy of them.
      Altruism is a virtue all too few people possess.
  altruism *n.*

am-bi-ent *adj.*   *Pronunciation:* ăm′byĕnt
  Meaning: lying in the area around, encompassing, en-
              veloping, enclosing
  Derivation: Latin *ambiens*, pres. part. of *ambire,* to go
              round
  Examples:
      The lecturer pointed out Turner's ambient light in
      his later paintings, which now hang in the Tate
      Museum.
      She showed me how the ambience in the painting
      contributed to the meaning of the work.
  ambience or ambiance *n.*

am-biv-a-lence *n.*   *Pronunciation:* ăm-bĭv′ă-lĕns
  Meaning: simultaneously repelling and attracting a
              person, object, or action
  Derivation: Latin *ambi*, both + *valens,* strength
  Examples:
      The ambivalence she felt toward him prompted her
      to delay any decision about his proposal.

What caused him to be so ambivalent about school was a mystery to everyone.

ambivalent *adj.*, ambivalently *adv.*

a-mel-io-rate *v.t., v.i.*   *Pronunciation:* ă-mēl′yŭ-rāt
  Meaning: *v.t.* to better, improve, reform, correct, mitigate; *v.i.* to grow better
 Derivation: Latin *ad*, to + *meliorare*, to make better
 Examples:
    v.t.   Despite his best efforts, he did not ameliorate the situation.
    v.i.   Conditions can be bettered, but the general condition will not ameliorate.

a-me-na-ble *adj.*   *Pronunciation:* ă-mē′nă-bl
  Meaning: responsive, submissive, yielding; liable, exposed
 Derivation: French *amener*, to bring to, conduct, lead; to fetch
 Examples:
    The author was not amenable to the slightest revision of his novel.
    He had an amenable nature, which is the reason that she stayed with him so long.
    Most politicians find themselves amenable to criticism once they come into prominence.

a-mor-al *adj.*   *Pronunciation:* ā-mŏr′ŭl
  Meaning: without a sense of moral responsibility, outside the realm in which moral distinctions are made

Derivation: Latin *a*, without + *moralis,* moral
Examples:
> Although many people are atheists, we must not think they are amoral.
>
> His amoral behavior shocked all who knew him well.

amorality *n.,* amorally *adv.*

a-mor-phous *adj.*   *Pronunciation:* ă-môr′fŭs
Meaning: without definite shape or structure, formless, unfashioned
Derivation: Greek *ámorphos* from *a* + *morphe,* without form
Examples:
> The amorphous nature of the design resulted in a building without appeal or utility.
>
> The symphony was so amorphous that the audience grew restless.

amorphousness *n.,* amorphously *adv.*

an-drog-y-nous *adj.*   *Pronunciation:* ăn-drŏj′ĭ-nŭs
Meaning: bisexual, having both male and female characteristics
Derivation: Greek *andrógynos,* hermaphroditic, both male and female
Examples:
> Samuel Taylor Coleridge wrote, "The truth is, a great mind must be androgynous."

Legislation to define the status of an androgynous person has yet to be enacted.

androgyny *n.*

a-nom-a-lous *adj.*   *Pronunciation:* ă-nŏm′ă-lŭs
  Meaning: deviating from the common; eccentric, irregular
Derivation: Greek *anomalos,* irregular
Examples:
  This kind of anomalous behavior will end in tragedy.
  Cyclones are weather anomalies.
anomaly and anomalousness *n.,* anomalously *adv.*

a-plomb *n.*   *Pronunciation:* ă-plŏm′
  Meaning: self-confidence, poise, self-assurance
Derivation: French *à,* according to + *plomb,* plummet
Examples:
  She always had more aplomb than most of her friends, and many of them resented it.
  For a young person, his aplomb was remarkable.

ar-ro-gant *adj.*   *Pronunciation:* ă′rō-gănt
  Meaning: assuming too much, insolent, haughty, overbearing
Derivation: Latin *arrogare,* to ask; to claim

Examples:
>   Arrogant behavior in the young is particularly offensive.
>
>   I will not countenance arrogance in my associates.

arrogance *n.,* arrogantly *adv.*

as-cet-ic *n., adj.*   *Pronunciation:* ă-sĕt′ĭk
>   *Meaning:* *n.* a person who practices rigorous self-denial; *adj.* practicing self-denial, austere

Derivation:
>   Greek *askētikós,* pertaining to a monk or hermit

Examples:
>   *n.* Ascetics are said to find their reward in contemplating eternal values.
>
>   *adj.* In our age, the ascetic life is out of place.

asceticism *n.,* ascetically *adv.*

as-in-ine *adj.*   *Pronunciation:* ăs′ĭ-nīn
>   *Meaning:* stupid, silly, like an ass
>   *Derivation:*   Latin *asinīnus,* ass
>   *Examples:*

>   The discussion was so asinine that half the audience left in disgust.
>
>   If you behave like an ass, you deserve to be called asinine.

asininity *n.,* asininely *adv.*

as-sid-u-ous *adj.*   *Pronunciation:* ă-sĭd′ū′ŭs
>   *Meaning:* persistent, devoted, attentive; constant in application; unflagging, zealous

Derivation: Latin *assidūus* from *assidēre,* to sit near.

Examples:

He is not the most assiduous student I have ever met.

I wish I were as assiduous as she; I would get higher grades.

assiduity and assiduousness *n.,* assiduously *adv.*

as-sim-i-late *v.t., v.i.*   *Pronunciation:* ă-sĭm′ĭ-lāt

Meaning: *v.t.* to make like, absorb; *v.i.* to become similar

Derivation: Latin *assimilātus* from *assimilāre,* to make like

Examples:

v.t. Food is assimilated in the body.

v.t. Truth cannot be assimilated by the crowd; it must propagate by contagion.

v.i. Aborigines are assimilating into modern life so rapidly that their cultures are in danger of disappearing.

assimilation *n.,* assimilative *adj.*

as-suage *v.t.*   *Pronunciation:* ă-swāj

Meaning: to ease, soften, mitigate; to appease, pacify, alleviate

Derivation: Latin *ad,* to + *suāvis,* sweet

Examples:

He looked for a fresh running stream to assuage his thirst.

Helena was not going to be assuaged by that explanation.

Feelings of guilt are finally assuaged by acts of expiation.

as-tute *adj.*   *Pronunciation:* ăs-tūt′
  Meaning: sagacious, wily, acute, discerning, keen
Derivation: Latin *astūtus* from *astūs,* crafty
  Examples:

The more astute your suggestions, the further you will advance.

They both had astute minds, which made them delightful companions.

astuteness *n.,* astutely *adv.*

at-ro-phy *v.t., v.i.*   *Pronunciation:* ăt′rō-fē
  Meaning: *v.t.* to cause to waste away from disuse or lack of nourishment; *v.i.* to deteriorate from disuse
Derivation: Greek *atrophia,* without nourishment
  Examples:

v.t. Organs are strengthened by nourishment and atrophied by disuse.

v.i. Muscles atrophy when they are not exercised regularly.

atrophy *n.,* atrophied *adj.*

a-ver-sion *n.*   *Pronunciation:*   ă-vûr′zhŭn
  Meaning: dislike, repugnance, antipathy
Derivation: Latin *aversio* from *āvertere,* to turn away
Examples:

    She had a marked aversion to any loud music.
    Jack thought that anyone who could tolerate opera
    would have no aversion to chamber music.

averse *adj.*

a-vert *v.t.*   *Pronunciation:*   ă-vûrt′
  Meaning: to ward off, turn aside, prevent
Derivation: Latin *āvertere,* to turn away
Examples:

    Prayer and penitence will avert the wrath of God.
    He averted his eyes during the eclipse in order to
    avoid blindness.

ax-i-o-matic *adj.*   *Pronunciation:*   ăk-sē-ō-măt′ĭk
  Meaning: self-evident
Derivation: Greek *axiōma* from *axioun,* to think worthy
Examples:

    It is axiomatic that all who are associated with the
    project will be aware of its importance.
    The camaraderie of men in military service is
    axiomatic.

axiom *n.,* axiomatically *adv.*

b B b

ba-nal *adj.*   *Pronunciation:*   bā′năl, bă-năl′
   Meaning: lacking in freshness and vigor, common-
place, trite, flat
Derivation: French *ban,* an ordinance
   Examples:
He uttered the most banal remarks as if they were
gems of wisdom.
That kind of banality will get you no place in the
literary world.
banality *n.,* banally *adv.*

bas-tion *n.*   *Pronunciation:* băs′chŭn

    Meaning: a fortification; a work projection from the main enclosure, having two faces and two flanks

Derivation: French from Italian *bastire,* to build

    Examples:

      Their failure to storm the bastion was unexplainable.

      The distant mountains appear impregnable bastions to the untrained eye.

      Some believe the United States to be the bastion of democracy.

bel-li-cose *adj.*   *Pronunciation:* běl-ĭ-kōs′

    Meaning: warlike, inclined to strife, aggressive

Derivation: Latin *bellicōsus* from *bellum,* war

    Examples:

      His bellicose behavior resulted in many arguments.

      These bellicose acts are denounced regularly in the United Nations.

bellicosity *n.,* bellicosely *adv.*

bel-lig-er-ent *adj.*   *Pronunciation:* bĕ-lĭj′ĕr-ĕnt

    Meaning: waging war, hostile, truculent

Derivation: Latin *belligerans,* to be at war

Examples:
> Such belligerent attitudes make peace almost un-
> attainable.
>
> Belligerent politicians are not scrupulous about the
> language they employ in condemning their
> enemies.

belligerence *n.,* belligerently *adv.*

bi-zarre *adj.*   *Pronunciation:* bĭ-zär′
  Meaning: odd, eccentric, full of incongruities
Derivation: Spanish *bizarro,* gallant
  Examples:
> These bizarre incidents are symptomatic of more
> serious flaws in our legal system.
>
> The novel was simply ordinary, striving to be
> bizarre.

bizarreness *n.,* bizarrely *adv.*

bla-tant *adj.*   *Pronunciation:* blā′tŭnt
  Meaning: clamorous, noisy; offensively obtrusive,
           coarse; loud
Derivation: The word blatant was invented by Edmund
           Spenser in *The Fairie Queene* (1596).
  Examples:
> She made a blatant attempt to arouse his attention.
>
> A blatant noise arose behind them, distracting
> their attention from the motion picture screen.

blatancy *n.,* blatantly *adv.*

buf-foon *n.*   *Pronunciation:* bŭ-f͞oon′
   Meaning: clown, one who indulges in low jests; one
              who uses ludicrous gestures.
Derivation: French *bouffon,* jester
  Examples:

     Sometimes one must play the buffoon to attain
     one's ambition.

     The short stories were nothing but a jumble of buf-
     foonery.

buffoonery *n.*

c C c

ca-coph-o-ny *n.*   *Pronunciation:* ka-kŏf′ŭ-nē

  Meaning: harsh or discordant sound, discordance, dissonance

Derivation: Greek *kakophonia,* bad sounding

  Examples:

    The mixture of the voices and the drums produced a horrible cacophony.

    Cacophonous winds swirled about them, driving them to the edge of madness.

cacophonous *adj.,* cacophonously *adv.*

cal-lous *adj.*   *Pronunciation:* kăl′ŭs
  Meaning: hardened in feeling, insensible, indifferent
  Derivation: Latin *callōsus,* thick-skinned
  Examples:
> His calloused hands were testimonials to his hard work.
> The callous behavior of public officials was inexcusable.

callus and callousness *n.,* callously *adv.*

ca-ma-ra-de-rie *n.*   *Pronunciation:* kă-mă-rä′dĕ-rē
  Meaning: good fellowship, good will between comrades
  Derivation: French *camaraderie,* fellowship
  Examples:
> Camaraderie usually exists among members of an athletic team.
> Her easy-going camaraderie was one of her most charming characteristics.

can-tan-ker-ous *adj.* *Pronunciation:*   kăn-tăng′kŭr-ŭs
  Meaning: ill-natured, perverse, contentious
  Derivation: Middle English *contek,* contention.
  Examples:
> My piano teacher was the most cantankerous person I ever knew.
> The donkey is a cantankerous and obstinate animal.

cantankerousness *n.,* cantankerously *adv.*

ca-pri-cious *adj.*   *Pronunciation:* kă-prĭsh'ŭs
   Meaning: an abrupt change in feeling or opinion
   Derivation: Italian *capriccio,* horror
   Examples:
      The defendant's refusal was not capricious but re-
      sulted from a serious concern over his rights.
      The boat responded to the capricious nature of the
      water.
caprice and capriciousness *n.,* capriciously *adv.*

cas-ti-gate *v.t.*   *Pronunciation:* kăs'ti-gāt
   Meaning: to punish, reprove, criticize severely; to cor-
               rect by severe corporal punishment, chas-
               tise, whip, flog
   Derivation: Latin *castigātus,* past part. *castigāre,* to cor-
               rect
   Examples:
      The teacher castigated her pupils until some of
      them revolted.
      The prison supervisor was told not to castigate pris-
      oners under any circumstances.
castigation and castigator *n.*

ca-thar-sis *n.*   *Pronunciation:* kă-thär'sĭs
   Meaning: purification of the emotions by art; purga-
               tive, cleansing
   Derivation: Greek *kátharsis,* purification, cleaning
   Examples:
      Aristotle felt the effect of tragedy was a catharsis of
      the emotions.

Psychoanalysts encourage discharge of hostile feelings through cathartic role-playing.

cathartic *n., adj.*

cha-grin *n., v.t.*   *Pronunciation:* shǎ-grĭn′
   Meaning: *n.* mental uneasiness caused by failure, disappointment, or humbled pride; mortification; *v.t.* to cause anguish by disappointment or humiliation (chiefly in the passive)
Derivation: French *chagraigner,* to grieve
Examples:
   n. The frustration of being thwarted was worse than the chagrin I felt.
   v.t. He was chagrined when he learned that he was not to be appointed as his manager's successor.

chiv-al-rous *adj.*   *Pronunciation:* shĭv′ăl-rŭs
   Meaning: courteous, attentive, gallant, noble
Derivation: French *chevalier,* knight
Examples:
   Helen is the most chivalrous person I know.
   The knight's chivalrous behavior was commented on by the court.

chivalrousness *n.,* chivalrously *adv.*

cir-cu-i-tous *adj.*   *Pronunciation:* sŭr-kū′ĭ-tŭs
   Meaning: roundabout, indirect
Derivation: Latin *circuitus,* abounding in roundabout courses.

Examples:

We had to use a circuitous route to avoid the bogs.

Betty had an artificial and circuitous way of speaking that masked a first-rate mind.

circuitousness *n.*, circuitously *adv.*

co-gent *adj.*   *Pronunciation:* cō′jĕnt

Meaning: convincing, appealing strongly to the mind or reason, compelling belief

Derivation: Latin *cōgere,* to compel

Examples:

Her cogent remarks convinced the skeptics.

I have two cogent reasons for not listing the subscribers.

cogency *n.*, cogently *adv.*

cog-ni-tion *n.*   *Pronunciation:* cŏg-nĭsh′ūn

Meaning: knowledge or the capacity for it, understanding, the faculty of perceiving or knowing

Derivation: Latin *cognitio,* becoming acquainted with

Examples:

Louise is always wrapped up in her reading but actually shows little cognition.

As a psychologist, he specialized in the problems associated with cognition.

cognitive *adj.*

cog-ni-zant *adj.*   *Pronunciation:* kŏg′nĭ-zănt
   Meaning: having   knowledge,   understanding,   or
              awareness
Derivation: Latin *cognoscere,* to know
Examples:
   The student was made cognizant of all his errors
   by his teachers.

   These writers were perfectly cognizant of all social
   problems but had little to offer by way of solutions.

co-here *v.i.*   *Pronunciation:*   kō-hēr′
   Meaning: to stick together; to be logically consistent;
              to be connected by a common principle.
Derivation: Latin *cohaerēre,* to adhere
Examples:
   The fragmentary accounts neither cohere nor
   satisfy, so we must await amplification.

   Because good writers are always coherent, they
   can be understood readily.
coherence *n.,* coherent *adj.*

col-lu-sion *n.*   *Pronunciation:* kō-lōō′zhŭn
   Meaning: deceit, fraud; a secret agreement for fraudu-
              lent purposes.
Derivation: Latin *collūsio,* playing together
Examples:
   The defense attorney accused the witness of collu-
   sion with the prosecution to entrap his client.

   Collusion is punished as severely as most felonies.
collusiveness *n.,* collusive *adj.,* collusively *adv.*

come-ly *adj.*   *Pronunciation:* kŭm'lē
   Meaning: pleasing to the eye, pleasant, becoming
Derivation: Anglo-Saxon *cȳmlic* from *cȳme,* beautiful
Examples:
      She was as comely as any woman I had ever seen.
      He had always thought of her as one of the come-
      liest women he had ever known, although he did not
      think her beautiful.
comeliness *n.*

com-punc-tion *n.*   *Pronunciation:*   kŏm-pŭngk'shŭn
   Meaning: uneasy sense of guilt; remorse; transient
                feeling of regret for a minor wrong
Derivation: Latin *com,* jointly + *pungere,* to prick, sting
Examples:
      He signed the letter of accusation without the least
      compunction.
      You might have thought they would have some
      compunction about committing the fraud.
compunctious *adj.*

con-gen-ial *adj.*   *Pronunciation:*   kŏn-jēn'yăl
   Meaning: kindred in tastes, opinions, or temperament;
                compatible, suitable
Derivation: Latin *congenialis,* alike in spirit
Examples:
      This soil is congenial to growing roses.
      She is the most congenial person I know, although
      at times she can show anger.
congeniality *n.,* congenially *adv.*

con-gen-i-tal *adj.*   *Pronunciation:*   kŏn-jĕn′ĭ-tĭl
  Meaning: existing at or dating from birth; belonging to
         one from birth.
  Derivation: Latin *congenitus,* born together with
  Examples:
     Congenital diseases are a common cause of illness
     in children.
     We must not confuse congenital conditions with
     imperfections resulting from heredity.
congenitally *adv.*

con-ten-tious *adj.*   *Pronunciation:*   kŏn-tĕn′shŭs
  Meaning: argumentative, quarrelsome
  Derivation: Latin *contentiōsus* from *contentio,* to con-
         tend
  Examples:
     We all felt that it was best if no contentious re-
     marks were made during the meeting.
     I don't think I would have been so contentious if
     someone had been there to restrain me.
contentiousness and contention *n.,* contentiously *adv.*

con-viv-i-al *adj.*   *Pronunciation:*   kŏn-vĭv′ĭ-āl
  Meaning: jovial, festive, gay; relating to eating and
         drinking in jovial fellowship
  Derivation: Latin *convīviālis,* pertaining to a feast

Examples:
> He suggested that one of the few redeeming features of being in the armed forces is the convivial atmosphere you encounter when you are on leave.
> She seemed to be in such a convivial mood that I feared to shatter it by telling her how late we were.

conviviality *n.*, convivially *adv.*

cov-ert *adj.*   *Pronunciation:*   kŭ′vĕrt, kō′vĕrt
 Meaning: sheltered, hidden, secret, private
Derivation: Old French, past part. *covrir,* to cover
 Examples:
> She took me to a covert nook in the garden.
> Most of the intelligence agencies in the world regularly engage in covert activities.

covertness *n.*, covertly *adv.*

cov-et *v.t.*   *Pronunciation:*   kŭv′ĭt
 Meaning: to desire, long for, wish for eagerly
Derivation: Old French *cuveitier,* from Latin *cupiditas,* desire
 Examples:
> *v.t.* Marcella coveted the sable coat, knowing she could never afford to buy it.
> *v.t.* Thou shalt not covet thy neighbor's wife.

covetousness *n.*, covetous *adj.*, covetously *adv.*

cul-pa-ble *adj.*   *Pronunciation:*   kŭl′pă-bl
 Meaning: deserving of censure or blame

Derivation: Old French *coupable,* culpable from Latin *culpare,* to blame
Examples:

In this instance, he seemed to be the most culpable of those who had been caught by the monitor.

Even though the student was not innocent, the dean felt that only those culpable in the extreme should be expelled.

culpability and culpableness *n.,* culpably *adv.*

cur-so-ry *adj.*   *Pronunciation:*   kŭr′sŭ-rē
Meaning: rapidly, often superficially performed when exhaustive treatment is needed
Derivation: Latin *cursōrius,* pertaining to a runner
Examples:

She gave the first file only a cursory examination and passed it on.

If she feels that she can assimilate all that information in a cursory glance, she is mistaken.

cursoriness *n.,* cursorily *adv.*

cy-no-sure *n.*   *Pronunciation:*   sī′nŭ-shoor
Meaning: center of attention, central point of interest, pole star
Derivation: Greek *kynósoura,* dog's tail
Examples:

The half-naked girl became the cynosure of all eyes.

Because of her beauty, she was the cynosure wherever she went, much to the distress of other women.

d D d

de-ca-dence *n.*　*Pronunciation:*　dĕ-kā′dĕns, dĕ′kŭ-dĕns

　Meaning:　quality or state of falling into decay; decline from a superior state, standard, or time; degeneration.

Derivation:　Latin *de,* down + *cadere,* to fall.

　Examples:

　　Decadence in art is not always recognized readily but the symptoms of decay will finally emerge.

　　Even nineteenth century French literature experienced a decadent period.

decadent *adj.,* decadently *adv.*

dec-i-mate *v.t.*   *Pronunciation:* dĕ'sĭ-māt
  Meaning: to destroy a large part of
  Derivation: Latin *decimatus,* past part. of *decimare,* to
           reduce by one-tenth
  Examples:

> If the examiner's intention was to decimate the class, he succeeded; many students will not return next semester.
>
> The decimation of the island's population was evident everywhere.

decimation, *n.*

de-lec-ta-tion *n.*   *Pronunciation:* dē-lĕk-tā'shŭn
  Meaning: delight, pleasure, enjoyment, gratification, joy
  Derivation: Latin *dēlectare,* to delight, please
  Examples:

> The child's delectation was obvious on Christmas morning.
>
> She prepared a delectable meal for him within minutes.

delectable *adj.,* delectably *adv.*

del-e-te-ri-ous *adj.*   *Pronunciation:* dĕl-ĕ-tē'rē-ŭs
  Meaning: destructive, harmful, unwholesome, pernicious
  Derivation: Latin *dēlētērius,* hurt, damaged

Examples:

Deleterious behavior shocks society but is soon forgotten.

If they cannot understand the deleterious nature of their relationship, they will never be able to improve it.

deleteriousness *n.*, deleteriously *adv.*

de-lin-e-ate *v.t.*   *Pronunciation:* dĭ-lĭn′e-āt

Meaning: to portray, depict, represent, sketch, draw, describe

Derivation: Latin *dēlīneātus,* marked out

Examples:

The instructor delineated the entire course during the first day of the class.

If you delineate your complaint adequately, you will at least get a ruling.

delineation *n.*

de-mean *v.t.*   *Pronunciation:* dĭ-mēn′

Meaning: to behave, conduct oneself; to degrade, debase, humble

Derivation: Old French *demener,* to conduct, manage

Examples:

I did not think that you would demean yourself in that manner.

Hiter's actions demeaned all of us.

From your demeanor, I can see that you are pleased with yourself, but I cannot understand why.

demeanor *n.*

den-i-grate *v.t.*   *Pronunciation:* dĕn′ĭ-grāt
  Meaning: to sully, defame
Derivation: Latin *denigrare,* to blacken
Examples:
> They were praised so faintly that it was obvious the speaker intended to denigrate them.
> The report was nothing more than a denigration of the entire project.

denigration and denigrator *n.*

den-i-zen *n.*   *Pronunciation:* dĕn′ĭ-zĕn
  Meaning: inhabitant; one naturalized in any society, fellowship, or region (often applied to animals)
Derivation: Old French *denzein,* one living within (as in a city)
Examples:
> Such people are denizens of our courts, despite all our efforts to assist them.
> Some people believe that there are denizens of the deep that will never be seen.

de-plore *v.t.*   *Pronunciation:* dĭ-plôr′
  Meaning: to lament, sorrow over, grieve for
Derivation: Latin, *deplorare,* to cry out, lament
Examples:
> Top management deplored the lack of response from the workers.
> While they deplored the decision, they decided to go along with it.

deplorable *adj.,* deplorably *adv.*

dep-re-cate *v.t.*   *Pronunciation:*   dĕp'rĭ-kāt
  Meaning: to disapprove of
  Derivation: Latin, *dēprecātus*, past part. of *dēprecāri*, to
              avert by prayer
  Examples:
      If you persist in these attempts to deprecate his
      character, I shall leave the room.
      Their behavior was deprecated by all present, in the
      belief that the couple had acted badly.
deprecation *n.*, deprecatingly *adv.*

de-ri-sion *n.*   *Pronunciation:*   dĭ-rĭ'zhŭn
  Meaning: act of scorning; object of scorn
  Derivation: Latin *dērīdere*, to laugh
  Examples:
      They greeted his speech with noisy derision.
      Such derisive behavior has no place in the class-
      room.
deride *v.t.*, derisive *adj.*

de-rog-a-tory *adj.*   *Pronunciation:*   dĭ-rŏg'ŭ-tō-rē
  Meaning: disparaging, detracting, of low estimate
              (said of a word or a usage)
  Derivation: Latin *dērogātus*, past part. of *dērogare*, to
              ask
  Examples:
      Paula was an expert in the use of derogatory
      phrases to hurt her debating opponents.
      Professor Low found more derogatory words and
      phrases in my paper than he thought appropriate.

Why must you derogate people who bear you no grudge?

derogation *n.*, derogate *v.t.*, *v.i.*, derogative *adj.*, derogatorily and derogatively *adv.*

des-pi-ca-ble *adj.*　　　　*Pronunciation:*　děs′pĭ-cŭ-bl

Meaning:　fit and deserving to be despised, contemptible

Derivation:　Latin *dēspicābilis* from *dēspicāri,* to despise

Examples:

Rape is one of the most despicable crimes committed by man.

Because of his despicable reputation, he made no friends at the club.

despicability and despicableness *n.*, despicably *adv.*

des-ul-to-ry *adj.*　　　　*Pronunciation:*　děs′ŭl-tō-rē

Meaning:　aimless, jumping from one thing to another without logical order or connection, off course

Derivation:　Latin *dēsultōrius* from *dēsultor,* a leaper

Examples:

The desultory negotiations inflamed the workers and prolonged the strike.

The debater failed to make his point because his desultory argument used up all his allotted time.

desultoriness *n.*, desultorily *adv.*

de-trac-tion *n.*   *Pronunciation:* dē-trăk'shŭn
  Meaning: slander, disparagement, calumny, belittle-
              ment, defamation
Derivation: Latin *de,* from + *trahere,* to draw
  Examples:
          The judge reprimanded both attorneys for their fre-
          quent detractions.
          Their efforts to detract from his reputation as a
          scholar were fruitless.
  detractor *n.,* detract *v.t.,* detractive and detractory *adj.*

di-aph-a-nous *adj.*   *Pronunciation:*   dī-ăf'ŭ-nŭs
  Meaning: transparent (said of a fabric)
Derivation: Middle Latin *diaphanus* from Greek
              diaphānes, transparent
  Examples:
          The diaphanous cloud floated lazily across the sky,
          scarcely casting a shadow below.
          A spider's web is so diaphanous that most insects do
          not see it.
  diaphanousness *n.,* diaphanously *adv.*

di-a-tribe *n.*   *Pronunciation:* dī' ă-trīb
  Meaning: a prolonged and heated discussion, bitter or
              abrasive discourse
Derivation: Latin *diatriba,* a learned discussion
  Examples:
          Every time you asked Jim a question, you received
          a diatribe.

She told him, "If you can't stop these diatribes, I'm leaving."

di-chot-o-my *n.*   *Pronunciation:* dī-kŏt′-ŭ-mē

Meaning: a cutting in two, a division into two subordinate parts

Derivation: Greek *dichotomīa,* a cutting in two

Examples:

The dichotomy between idealism and materialism in the modern world is apparent to all social scientists.

This was the kind of dichotomy he was trying to avoid, since there would be no way of repairing it.

dichotomize *v.t., v.i.,* dichotomous *adj.,* dichotomously *adv.*

di-dac-tic *adj.*   *Pronunciation:* dī-dăk′tĭk

Meaning: instructive, intended to teach

Derivation: Greek *didaktikōs* from *didaskein,* to teach

Examples:

Almost all the tales in the collection were didactic in tone, so students disliked them.

She was by nature a didactic person, always attempting to teach by example.

didacticism *n.,* didactically *adv.*

dil-a-to-ry *adj.*   *Pronunciation:* dĭl′ŭ-tō-rē

Meaning: tardy, slow, causing delay, tending to procrastinate

Derivation: Late Latin *dilātōrius* from *dilātor,* a de-
                layer.

Examples:

The dilatory nonchalance of both sides was annoy-
ing to us, for we had precious little time to spare.

John's dilatory nature was troublesome to most of
his friends.

dilatoriness *n.,* dilatorily *adv.*

dil-i-gent *adj.*   *Pronunciation:*   dĭl'ŭ-jĕnt
    Meaning: industrious, assiduous, careful
Derivation: Latin *dīligens,* pres. part. of *dīlengere,* to
                choose; to like

Examples:

He was diligent enough in his studies to make the
dean's list.

Diligence and ambition often lead to accumulation
of wealth.

diligence *n.,* diligently *adv.*

dis-cern *v.t.*   *Pronunciation:*   dĭ-zûrn', dĭ-sûrn'
    Meaning: to understand, detect; to judge, decide be-
                tween
Derivation: Latin *discernere,* to distinguish
    Examples:

Frances had the ability to discern right from wrong
in most situations.

If he had any ability on the basketball court, it was
not discernible on this occasion.

My mother showed discernment in handling family disputes.

The art critic was noted for his discerning eye.

discernment *n.*, discernible and discerning *adj.*

dis-con-so-late *adj.*   *Pronunciation:*   dĭs-kŏn′sō-lĭt
  Meaning: deeply dejected, sad, hopeless
Derivation: Latin *dis,* apart + *consolātus,* past part. of
        consolāri, to console
  Examples:

The youths were disconsolate over the loss of the football game.

If one observes carefully, one can become disconsolate over the condition of the nation's schools.

disconsolately *adv.*

dis-course *n.*   *Pronunciation:*   dĭs′kôrs, dĭs-kôrs′
  Meaning: communication of thought through words
Derivation: French *discours,* discussion
  Examples:

Sometimes the effectiveness of discourse depends on the speaker's vocabulary and the temper of his mind.

The discourse was brief and incisive, but the audience seemed restless.

discourse *v.*

dis-cur-sive *adj.*   *Pronunciation:*   dĭs-kĕr′sĭv
  Meaning: digressive, rambling, wandering away from the subject, not sticking to the point

Derivation: Latin *discurrere,* to run away
Examples:
> Whenever she stopped consulting her notes, her talk became discursive and boring.

> A discursive speech usually results from lack of preparation.

discursiveness *n.,* discursively *adv.*

dis-in-gen-u-ous *adj.*   *Pronunciation:*   dĭs-ĭn-jĕn′ū-ŭs
Meaning: not frank or candid, deceitful, insincere
Derivation: Latin *dis,* apart + *ingenuus,* inborn, freeborn; noble; frank
Examples:
> The intent of that letter was thoroughly disingenuous.

> The Secretary of State was considered disingenuous by members of the committee.

disingenuousness *n.,* disingenuously *adv.*

dis-mal *adj.*   *Pronunciation:*   dĭz′mŭl
Meaning: cheerless, depressing
Derivation: perhaps from Latin *diēs malī,* bad days
Examples:
> That was a dismal presentation to make before so young an audience.

> He was so ashamed of his dismal performance that he threw the ball over the fence.

dismalness *n.,* dismally *adv.*

dis-par-age *v.t.*   *Pronunciation:* dĭs-păr'ĭj
  Meaning: to speak of in a slighting way, treat with
            contempt
  Derivation: Old French *desparagier,* to match unequally
  Examples:

    I think the news media have disparaged his per-
    formance long enough.

    She hoped fervently that she would be treated fairly
    and not be disparaged before she could offer an
    explanation.

disparager and disparagement *n.,* disparaging *adj.,* dis-
paragingly *adv.*

dis-pa-rate *adj.*   *Pronunciation:* dĭs'pă-rĭt
  Meaning: unequal, dissimilar; radically different
  Derivation: Latin *disparare,* to part
  Examples:

    The two sisters are so disparate in nature that they
    ought to stay away from each other.

    Consistently disparate opinions made their long
    marriage interesting but fragile.

disparateness *n.,* disparately *adj.*

dis-so-nant *adj.*   *Pronunciation:* dĭs'ō-nănt
  Meaning: discordant, incongruous
  Derivation: Latin *dissonare,* to disagree in sound

Examples:

> The band made such dissonant sounds that the au-
> dience departed in disgust.

> Dissonant tones are unrelated, unorganized, and
> rarely useful in conventional music.

dissonance *n.,* dissonantly *adv.*

dis-tort *v.t.*   *Pronunciation:* dĭs-tôrt′
Meaning: to twist, warp; to pervert; to pull out of shape
Derivation: Latin *distorquere,* to twist out of shape
Examples:

> Unwilling to hear the truth, the policeman dis-
> torted my answer and took me off to headquarters.

> The defense of a policy of armed intervention rested
> on a weak foundation of distortions and half-truths.

distortion *n.,* distorted *adj.,* distortedly *adv.*

di-vulge *v.t.*   *Pronunciation:* dĭ-vŭlj′
Meaning: to make public, reveal, disclose, make
               known
Derivation: Latin *divulgare,* to spread among the people
Examples:

> To divulge even this little story would be to ruin her
> reputation.

> Testimony at the trial divulged that the defendant
> had not been made aware of her rights at the time
> of arrest.

divulgence and divulger *n.*

du-bi-ous *adj.* *Pronunciation:* dū′bĭ-ŭs, doo′bĭ-ŭs
  Meaning: doubtful, open to suspicion
Derivation: Latin *dubiōsus* from *dubium,* doubt
Examples:

His dubious statements caused many to wonder about his sanity.

"Certainly I see the point," he said dubiously and proceeded on to another topic.

dubiousness *n.,* dubiously *adv.*

eEe

e-bul-li-ent *adj.* *Pronunciation:* ĭ-bŭl′ĭ-ĕnt, ĭ-bŭl′yĕnt

Meaning: showing excitement, overflowing with high spirits

Derivation: Latin *ēbulliens,* pres. part. of *ēbullire,* to boil up

Examples:

Susan's ebullient spirits gained her many friends.

The team was so ebullient over their victory that they dowsed each other with water from a hose.

ebullience *n.*

ed-i-fy *v.t.*   *Pronunciation:* ĕd′ĭ-fī

Meaning: to improve, instruct; to strengthen spiritually or morally especially by example

Derivation: Old French *edifier*, to teach

Examples:

The professor sought to edify his students by recounting stories of his early life.

If you were edified by his sermon, you might write Pastor Schmidt and let him know.

edification and edifier *n.*, edifyingly *adv.*

e-lic-it *v.t.*   *Pronunciation:* ĭ-lĭs′ĭt

Meaning: to draw out or forth; to evoke

Derivation: Latin *ēlicitus, past part. of ēlicere*, to draw out by coaxing

Examples:

They sought to elicit some response from the frightened child.

All that could be elicited from the interview was that the applicant was interested in the position.

elicitation and elicitor *n.*

e-lu-ci-date *v.t.*   *Pronunciation:* ĭ-lōo′sĭ-dāt

Meaning: to make clear or intelligible

Derivation: Late Latin *ēlucidātus*, full of light, clear

Examples:

I wish you would elucidate that statement sufficiently so that I can understand it.

The plan was elucidated by the use of charts and diagrams that illustrated every important detail.

elucidation and elucidator *n.*, elucidative *adj.*

em-a-nate *v.i.*   *Pronunciation:*   ĕm'ŭ-nāt
  Meaning: to issue from a source, flow out from
Derivation: Latin ēmānāre, to flow out
Examples:

> The subtle fragrance emanated from some unseen flowers planted nearby.
>
> The stream emanated from a spring far up in the hills.

emanative *adj.*

e-mas-cu-late *v.t.*   *Pronunciation:*   ĭ-măs'kyŭ-lāt
  Meaning: to deprive of masculine qualities or virility; castrate; to weaken
Derivation: Latin ēmasculāre, to castrate
Examples:

> Warren said he would resign rather than be an emasculated leader.
>
> Marriage to a woman like Phyllis must be an emasculative experience.

emasculation and emasculator *n.*, emasculative *adj.*

em-pa-thy *n.*   *Pronunciation:*   ĕm'pŭ-thē
  Meaning: projecting one's own consciousness into another person; appreciative understanding
Derivation: Greek *empátheia*, suffering
Examples:

> I felt a great deal of empathy for the actors performing on the stage.

Unless one has empathy, it is difficult to feel what other persons feel.

empathic *adj.*, empathically *adv.*

en-cum-ber *v.t.*   *Pronunciation:* ĕn-kŭm′bŭr
  Meaning: to place a burden upon; to load with debts
Derivation: Old French *encombrer,* to obstruct
  Examples:
      The expedition was encumbered with all sorts of unnecessary equipment.
      The firm was so encumbered with debts that no bank would finance it further.

encumbrance *n.*

e-nig-ma *n.*   *Pronunciation:* ĕ-nĭg′mŭ
  Meaning: an obscure saying, a riddle; something having no explanation
Derivation: Latin *aenigma,* riddle
  Examples:
      She always acts as though life were an enigma.
      If he allowed his actors to act like normal human beings, his plays would not be so enigmatic.

enigmatic and enigmatical *adj.*, enigmatically *adv.*

en-mi-ty *n.*   *Pronunciation:* ĕn′mĭ-tē
  Meaning: hatred, mutual antagonism, ill will
Derivation: Old French *ennemistie,* not friendly

Examples:

I had not realized there was so much enmity between them.

Persons who show so much enmity rarely make
lasting friendships.

e-qua-nim-i-ty *n.*   *Pronunciation:* ĕ-kwă-nĭm'ĭ-tē
   Meaning: evenness of mind or temper, calmness, com-
               posure
Derivation: Latin *aequanimitas,* of even mind
Examples:

Fred seems to have recovered his equanimity.

When one becomes engaged in an argument, it is
best to retain one's equanimity in order to keep the
dispute from exploding into something bigger.

e-quiv-o-cal *adj.*   *Pronunciation:* ĭ-kwĭv'ō-kl
   Meaning: capable of more than one meaning; ambigu-
               ous, inconclusive, ambivalent
Derivation: Late Latin *aequivocus,* ambiguous
Examples:

The equivocal nature of the evidence left the jury
with no alternative but to declare the defendant
innocent.

He was so equivocal in his answer that I realized he
had not read the text.

equivocation and equivocalness *n.,* equivocally *adv.*

es-chew *v.t.*   *Pronunciation:* ĕs-choo'
   Meaning: to shun, avoid

Derivation: Old French, *eschiver,* to shun, avoid

Examples:

>Observers thought the concern would eschew all connections with a product sure to lose money.

>If she did not eschew evil, at least she did not court it.

eschewal and eschewer *n.*

e-the-re-al *adj.*   *Pronunciation:* ĭ-thĭr′ĭ-ŭl

>*Meaning:* unusually refined and delicate; light, airy; tenuous

Derivation: Latin *aetherius,* pertaining to the ether

Examples:

>His ethereal bearing caused many to underestimate his strength.

>Joan's theories were so ethereal that they had no basis in facts.

ethereality and etherealness *n.,* ethereally *adv.*

eu-phor-ic *adj.*   *Pronunciation:* u-fôr′ic

>*Meaning:* condition of feeling well, sense of well being

Derivation: Greek *eúphoros,* bearing well

Examples:

>She was in such a euphoric state that no one could annoy her.

>This feeling of euphoria lasted only as long as the concert—then reality took over.

euphoria *n.,* euphoristic *adj.*

e-voke *v.t.*   *Pronunciation:* ĭ-vōk′
  Meaning: to summon forth; to call up
  Derivation: French *évoquer,* to call forth
  Examples:
    Sally's wan smile evoked feelings of tenderness in
    her father.
    During one of his many periods of temporary insan-
    ity, he attempted to evoke the devil.
  evocation *n.,* evocative *adj.*

ex-ac-er-bate *v.t.*   *Pronunciation:* ĕg-zăs′ĕr-bāt
  Meaning: to irritate, embitter; to render more violent
  Derivation: Latin *exacerbātus,* past part. of *exacerbāre,*
          to irritate
  Examples:
    Their action exacerbated the situation; all hope of
    an amicable solution seemed lost.
    This line of questions exacerbated the witness, and
    he refused to answer.
  exacerbation *n.*

ex-co-ri-ate *v.t.*   *Pronunciation:* ĕks-kō′rē-āt
  Meaning: to censure scathingly; to skin alive in words;
          to skin alive
  Derivation: Late Latin *excoriāre,* to strip the hide off
  Examples:
    Most of her classmates winced as the professor ex-
    coriated Ruth for a mistake they considered trivial.
    The early Christians were sometimes excoriated by
    the Romans.
  excoriation *n.*

ex-cul-pate *v.t.*　　　　　　*Pronunciation:*　ĕks′cŭl-pāt
　　Meaning:　to clear from alleged fraud or guilt, exoner
　　　　　　　ate
　Derivation:　Latin *exculpare,* to free from blame
　Examples:
　　　The lawyer managed to exculpate his client
　　　through skillful legal manipulation.
　　　Exculpatory testimony was given late in the trial,
　　　but the jury sat stone-faced and unhearing.
exculpation *n.,* exculpatory *adj.*

ex-e-cra-ble *adj.*　　　　*Pronunciation:*　ĕk′sĕ-krŭ-bl
　Meaning:　detestable, extremely bad, abominable
　Derivation:　Latin *execrābilis,* detestable
　Examples:
　　　Wanda had execrable taste in clothes.
　　　That was the most execrable meal I have ever
　　　tasted.
execrably *adv.*

ex-e-crate *v.t.*　　　　　*Pronunciation:*　ĕk′sĕ-krat
　Meaning:　to detest utterly, abhor; to curse
　Derivation:　Latin *execrāre,* to curse
　Examples:
　　　Those mild curses don't bother me; I've been exe
　　　crated by masters.
　　　Frances was ashamed that she had allowed herself
　　　to be execrated by someone as mean as Jean.
execration *n.*

ex-i-gent *adj.*   *Pronunciation:*   ĕxʹĭ-jĕnt
  Meaning: needing immediate aid or action; urgent,
              critical
  Derivation: Latin *exigens,* pres. part. of *exigere,* to drive
                  out
  Examples:
        The letter conveyed an exigent situation, so he re-
        sponded immediately.
        The bill was passed in a mood of great exigency.
  exigency *n.*

ex-ig-u-ous *adj.*   *Pronunciation:*   ĕg-zĭjʹū-ŭs
  Meaning: scanty, meager, slender
  Derivation: Latin *exiguus,* scanty
  Examples:
        Congress appropriated only exiguous amounts for
        the developing countries in order to determine
        where the money was going before granting larger
        amounts.
        The cabaret boasted nothing more than an exigu-
        ous dance floor the size of a postage stamp and a
        tired piano player.
  exiguousness and exiguity *n.*

ex-on-er-ate *v.t.*   *Pronunciation:*   ĕg-zŏnʹ ĕr-āt
  Meaning: to clear from blame, exculpate, free from a
              charge
  Derivation: Latin *exonerātus,* past part. of *exonerāre,* to
                  free from a burden

Examples:

> The judge exonerated the defendant when the defense produced its surprise witness.
>
> How can you expect to be exonerated when they have all that evidence against you?

exoneration *n.,* exonerative *adj.*

ex-pa-ti-ate *v.i.*   *Pronunciation:*   ĕks-pā′shĭ-āt

Meaning: to talk freely and at length; to speak or write copiously on a subject

Derivation: Latin *expateri,* to spread out

Examples:

> The professor expatiated on his favorite topic until half the class was asleep.
>
> If you hope to expatiate on that subject tonight, you had better check your notes.

expatiation and expatiator *n.*

ex-pos-tu-late *v.i.*   *Pronunciation:*   ĕks-pŏs′tū-lāt

Meaning: to reason seriously with a person; to remonstrate

Derivation: Latin *expostulātus,* past part. of *expostulāre,* to demand vehemently

Examples:

> We expostulated with them for four hours to no avail.
>
> His windy expostulations brought him no new support but rather caused him to lose votes.

ex-tri-cate *v.t.*   *Pronunciation:*   ĕks′trĭ-kāt
  Meaning: to free from difficulties, disentangle
Derivation: Latin *extrīcātus,* past part. of *extrīcāre,* to
                free from impediments or perplexities
  Examples:

      When he saw no chance to extricate himself from
      the charge, he jumped bail.

      Her friends sought to extricate Sally from her dif-
      ficulties by contributing to a fund that would pay
      her hospital bills.

f F f

fal-la-cious *adj.*   *Pronunciation:*   fă-lā′shŭs
  Meaning: false, misleading, deceptive
Derivation: Latin *fallācia,* deceit
  Examples:

No conclusion is more fallacious than that which rests on isolated facts.

This kind of fallacious reasoning is all too prevalent among undergraduates.

fallaciousness and fallacy *n.,* fallaciously *adv.*

fas-tid-i-ous *adj.*   *Pronunciation:*   făs-tĭd′ĭ-ŭs
  Meaning: delicate to a fault, overly nice; difficult to please
Derivation: Latin *fastīdiōsus*, loathful
Examples:
> Henry was fastidious in almost everything but not in dress.
>
> It is perfectly all right to be fastidious, but not in everything, all the time.

fastidiousness *n.*, fastidiously *adv.*

fat-u-ous *adj.*   *Pronunciation:* făch′ū-ŭs
  Meaning: foolish, inane, silly; unreal, illusory
Derivation: Latin *fatuus*, foolish
Examples:
> While they seemed to reason effectively, close analysis revealed that most of what they said was simply fatuous.
>
> Their promises of peace were good examples of diplomatic fatuousness.

fatuousness *n.*, fatuously *adv.*

fe-cund *adj.*   *Pronunciation:*   fē′cŭnd, fĕ′cŭnd
  Meaning: fruitful, fertile, prolific
Derivation: Latin *fecundus*, fruitful
Examples:
> The island was a paradise, fecund in all kinds of fruit and temperate in climate all through the year.

She was so fecund a wife that she produced a child a
year.

fecundity *n.*

fe-ro-cious *adj.*   *Pronunciation:*   fĕ-rō'shŭs
 Meaning: fierce, savage, rapacious
Derivation: Latin *ferox,* fierce
Examples:

The tiger is a ferocious hunter, feared throughout
the jungle.

Off the field she was sweet and gentle, on it her
ferocity knew no bounds.

ferocity and ferociousness *n.,* ferociously *adv.*

fer-vid *adj.*   *Pronunciation:*   fĕr' vĭd
 Meaning: ardent, zealous, vehement
Derivation: Latin *fervidus,* very hot
Examples:

The entire field was full of fervid activity.

She was the most fervid speaker of all the new
legislators.

fervor *n.,* fervidly *adv.*

fet-id *adj.*   *Pronunciation:*   fĕt'ĭd
 Meaning: having an offensive smell
Derivation: Latin *foetidus* from *foetere,* to stink

Examples:

The swamp gave off a fetid odor that kept people away.

Paper factories are well known for their fetidness.

fetidness *n.,* fetidly *adv.*

fi-as-co *n.*   *Pronunciation:* fē-ăs'kō
  Meaning: a complete failure
  Derivation: Italian *fiasco,* bottle
  Examples:

The entire affair was a fiasco from start to finish.

Another fiasco like this and the entire squad will work out afternoons.

flac-cid *adj.*   *Pronunciation:* flăk'sĭd
  Meaning: limp, flabby, soft and weak
  Derivation: Latin *flaccidus,* flabby
  Examples:

Americans are more flaccid than Europeans, according to many students of physical education.

The more flaccid one is, the more one needs exercise.

flaccidity and flaccidness *n.,* flaccidly *adv.*

flam-boy-ant *adj.*   *Pronunciation:* flăm-boī'ĭnt
  Meaning: florid, ornate, given to dashing display, showy

Derivation: French, pres. part. of *flamboyer,* to flame
Examples:

Her flamboyant dancing drew raves from the critics.

A flamboyant orator may keep his audience enthralled yet say little that will be remembered.

flamboyance and flamboyancy *n.,* flamboyantly *adv.*

flor-id *adj.*   *Pronunciation:* flôr´ĭd

Meaning: tinged with red, ruddy
Derivation: Latin *flōridus,* blooming
Examples:

Her florid complexion was matched by her red hair.

Walsh looked too florid to be healthy, too exuberant to be happy.

floridness *n.,* floridly *adv.*

for-tu-i-tous *adj.*   *Pronunciation:* fôr-tū´ĭ-tŭs

Meaning: occurring by chance, without deliberate intention
Derivation: Latin *fortuītus,* by chance
Examples:

Evolution is not fortuitous, but methodical.

She missed a chance for free opera tickets when she fortuitously overslept.

fortuitousness *n.,* fortuitously *adv.*

fren-et-ic *adj.*   *Pronunciation:*   frĭ-nĕt′ĭk
  Meaning: frenzied, frantic
Derivation: Middle English *frenetike,* insane
  Examples:
      The leader set such a frenetic pace that I could not
      keep up.
      Sandra's frenetic behavior seemed odd in a girl
      ordinarily calm.
frenetically *adv.*

friv-o-lous *adj.*   *Pronunciation:*   frĭv′ŭ-lŭs
  Meaning: of little weight or importance, slight
Derivation: Latin *frīvolus,* silly
  Examples:
      Matthew never did a frivolous thing in his life.
      Frivolousness should not be confused with wit.
      Frivolity makes for a good party on New Year's
      Eve.
frivolousness and frivolity *n.,* frivolously *adv.*

fru-gal *adj.*   *Pronunciation:*   froo′gl
  Meaning: economical, thrifty, provident
Derivation: Latin *frūgālis,* virtuous, frugal
  Examples:
      I thought she was more frugal than necessary.
      The Scots have a reputation for frugality.
frugality and frugalness *n.,* frugally *adv.*

fur-tive *adj.*   *Pronunciation:*   fĕr′ tĭv
   Meaning: done by stealth, secret
Derivation: Latin *furtum,* theft
Examples:

> His movements were furtive, like a dog that has stolen a bone.

> Weasels are very furtive animals, which may account for their success in the struggle for survival.

furtiveness *n.,* furtively *adv.*

fu-tile *adj.*   *Pronunciation:*   fyūt′l
   Meaning: serving no useful purpose, frivolous
Derivation: Latin *futilis,* pours out easily, useless
Examples:

> She discovered that talking in this throng was futile.

> Suicides see no promise in life, only futility.

futility and futileness *n.,* futilely *adv.*

g G g

gar-ish *adj.*   *Pronunciation:*   găr′ĭsh

   Meaning: showy, glaring, outlandish

Derivation: Early English *gare*, stare

Examples:

     Everyone thought she wore the most garish jewelry.

     The neon lights in front of the store window emphasized the garishness of its display.

garishness *n.*, garishly *adv.*

gar-ru-lous *adj.* *Pronunciation:* găr′ū-lŭs
 Meaning: long winded, diffuse, verbose
 Derivation: Latin *garrulus,* talkative
 Examples:
   The old woman became more and more garrulous as the shock wore off.
   As the semester progressed, the professor became tiresomely garrulous.
garrulousness *n.,* garrulously *adv.*

gaud-y *adj.* *Pronunciation:* gawd′e
 Meaning: of showy, ostentatious color; tasteless
 Derivation: Old French *gaude,* plant yielding yellow dye
 Examples:
   I don't think I could walk the streets in such gaudy clothing.
   They dressed gaudily in order to attract attention.
gaudiness *n.,* gaudily *adv.*

ges-tic-u-late *v.i.* *Pronunciation:* jĕs-tĭk′u-lāt
 Meaning: to make lively motions with the body, especially when speaking or attracting attention
 Derivation: Latin *gesticulātus,* past part. of *gesticulāri,* to gesticulate
 Examples:
   When I saw her last, she was gesticulating violently.
   As the speaker grew more and more agitated, his gesticulations became more and more pronounced.
gesticulation *n.,* gesticulatory *adj.*

glib *adj.*   *Pronunciation:* glĭb
  Meaning: speaking smoothly, flippant; smooth, slippery
  Derivation: Dutch *glibberib,* smooth
  Examples:
    His glib speech wasn't overlooked by the interviewer.
    Everyone found his glib manner distasteful, but no one thought enough of him to suggest that he change.
glibness *n.,* glibly *adv.*

goad *n., v.t.*   *Pronunciation:* gōd
  Meaning: *n.* anything that stings, incites, or spurs to action; a pointed stick; *v.t.* to drive, incite, arouse
  Derivation: Anglo-Saxon *gād,* spear, point, arrow
  Examples:
    n. The young farmer used a goad to keep his cattle from straying from the market.
    v.t. The instructor hoped to goad him into learning the lesson.

gra-tu-i-tous *adj.*   *Pronunciation:* grȧ-tū′ĭ-tŭs
  Meaning: given freely, without recompense or regardless of merit; not called for by the circumstances, unwarranted
  Derivation: Latin *grātuītus,* pleasing

Examples:

The sergeant was infuriated by the gratuitous remarks of his commanding officer.

She decided that his gratuitous insults could no longer be ignored.

gratuitousness *n.*, gratuitously *adv.*

gra-tu-i-ty *n.*   *Pronunciation:* gră-tū'ĭ-tē

Meaning: tip, payment for service for which no bill is offered

Derivation: Latin *grātuītus*, pleasing

Examples:

A gratuity of 10 to 15 percent of the check is customary in many restaurants.

Many cultures reject the practice of offering gratuities.

gre-gar-i-ous *adj.*   *Pronunciation:* grĕ-gär'ē-ŭs

Meaning: associating with or going together in groups or herds; pertaining to or affecting a flock, crowd, or community; sociable

Derivation: Latin *gregarius* from *grex, gregis,* herd

Examples:

The wolf is a gregarious animal, despite the expression "lone wolf."

As any sociology textbook will tell you, it is the exceptional person who is not gregarious.

gregariousness *n.*, gregariously *adv.*

gul-li-ble *adj.*   *Pronunciation:*   gŭl′ĭ-bl

  Meaning: capable of being duped, fooled; easily de-
           ceived

Derivation: Old French *gole,* throat, gullet

  Examples:

      Joan was a very gullible person, but no one took
      advantage of her.

      Gullibility is not usually found in a New York City
      policeman.

gullibility *n.,* gullibly *adv.*

h H h

hag-gard *adj.*   *Pronunciation:*   hăg′ērd

   Meaning: having the expression of one wasted by want, suffering, or anxiety; gaunt; worn and anxious in appearance

Derivation: Middle French *hagard,* wild

  Examples:

     After several days on a meager diet, they began to look haggard.

     His cheeks were haggard; hollow were his eyes.

haggardness *n.,* haggardly *adv.*

ha-rangue *n.*   *Pronunciation:* hă-răng′
  Meaning: a noisy, boisterous speech; a tirade
Derivation: French *harangue*
Examples:
> No one could call that harangue a speech, yet the crowd was deeply moved.
>
> He harangued the mob for twenty minutes, calling for decisive action with no further delay.

harangue *v.t., v.i.*

har-bin-ger *n.*   *Pronunciation:* här′bĭn-jĕr
  Meaning: forerunner, precursor
Derivation: Old French *herbergeor,* a provider of lodging
Examples:
> The robin is the harbinger of spring in many regions.
>
> The trimming of the Christmas tree is the harbinger of Yuletide festivities.

hei-nous *adj.*   *Pronunciation:* hā′nŭs
  Meaning: hateful, horribly bad, odious, atrocious
Derivation: Old French *hainos,* hateful
Examples:
> Murder is considered a heinous crime in every society.
>
> They were guilty of a heinous disregard of fundamental human rights.

heinousness *n.,* heinously *adv.*

her-maph-ro-dite *n.* *Pronunciation:* hŭr-măf′rō-dīt
  Meaning: having both male and female reproductive
          organs
  Derivation: Greek *hermaphródītos* from *Hermes* and
          Aphrodite
  Examples:
    Many mollusks and worms are hermaphrodites.
    A great number of flowering plants are hermaph-
    roditic.
hermaphroditic *adj.*, hermaphroditically *adv.*

het-er-o-ge-ne-ous *adj.* *Pronunciation:* hĕt-rō-jē′nĭ-yŭs
  Meaning: dissimilar, having unlike qualities
  Derivation: Greek *heterogenés,* of different kinds
  Examples:
    She presented the college with a large collection of
    heterogeneous writings.
    The bag was a heterogeneous collection of shirts,
    socks, shoes, and old newspapers.
heterogeneousness and heterogeneity *n.*, heterogene-
ously *adv.*

hom-i-ly *n.* *Pronunciation:* hŏm′ĭ-lē
  Meaning: a discourse or sermon, a long sermon on
          some moral point
  Derivation: Old French *omelie,* discourse

Examples:

The minister preached a tedious homily on original sin.

Not all homilies are tedious—some are plain dull.

homilist *n.,* homiletic *adj.*

ho-mo-ge-ne-ous *adj.   Pronunciation:*   hō-mō-jē′nē-ŭs
   Meaning: of the same kind or nature, similar, structurally alike
   Derivation: Middle Latin *homogeneus,* of the same kind
   Examples:

The soup had a perfectly homogeneous texture, which made it easy to swallow.

Sweden has a relatively homogeneous population.

homogeneousness and homogeneity *n.,* homogeneously *adv.*

hor-ren-dous *adj.   Pronunciation:*   hō-rĕn′dŭs
   Meaning: horrible, fearful, frightful, dreadful
   Derivation: Latin *horrendus,* bristling
   Examples:

Not going to the most important party of the year was an horrendous sacrifice for the young mother.

Although the critics raved about the play, she thought it was horrendous.

horrendously *adv.*

hy-poth-e-sis *n.*   *Pronunciation:* hī-pŏth'ĕ-sĭs

  Meaning: supposition, assumed premise, assumption; a tentative theory adopted to explain certain facts or theories

Derivation: Greek *hypothesis,* a foundation; base, groundwork

  Examples:

There was no basis in fact for the hypothesis he advanced to explain the curious phenomenon.

A topic sentence usually presents a hypothetical statement that the other sentences in the paragraph prove or disprove.

hypothesize *v.t., v.i.,* hypothetical *adj.*

i I i

i-con-o-clast *n.*   *Pronunciation:* ī-kŏn′ō-klăst

   Meaning: one who is destructive of traditional institu-
              tions; idol-breaker, image-destroyer

Derivation: Greek *eikon,* an image + *klan,* to break

   Examples:

      An iconoclast exposes false pretensions in order to
      stir men and women.

      H. L. Mencken was full of iconoclastic ideas, some of
      which remain shocking even today.

iconoclastic *adj.,* iconoclastically *adv.*

ig-no-min-i-ous *adj.*   *Pronunciation:* ĭg-no̅-mĭn′e̅-ŭs

  Meaning: dishonorable, shameful, scandalous, infamous

Derivation: Latin *igno̅minio̅sus,* of ill fame

  Examples:

    That ignominious decision against women's rights will be contested in the courts by the leadership of several civil rights organizations.

    How many suicides among young people can be traced to inability to face the ignominy of scholastic failure?

ignominy and ignominiousness *n.,* ignominiously *adv.*

il-lu-so-ry *adj.*   *Pronunciation:* ĭl-lu̅′so̅-re̅

  Meaning: deceptive, fallacious, unreal

Derivation: Latin *illu̅sus,* past part. of illu̅dere, to mock

  Examples:

    Success seemed as illusory as ever after twenty years' hard work.

    How long can we go on nourished only by illusions, never realizing any tangible rewards?

illusion and illusoriness *n.,* illusorily *adv.*

im-bue *v.t.*   *Pronunciation:* ĭm-bu̅′

  Meaning: to saturate, tinge deeply; to inspire

Derivation: Latin *imbuere,* to stain

  Examples:

    The cloth was imbued with herbs and spices, making it delightful to smell.

    The entire performance was imbued with grace and natural beauty.

im-mi-nent *adj.*   *Pronunciation:* ĭm′mĭ-nĕnt
  Meaning: occurring immediately, impending
  Derivation: Latin *imminens,* pres. part. of *imminere,* to
           project
  Examples:
     Disposition of the case is imminent, if we are to
     believe the newspapers.
     Some scientists believe that the solution to the
     problem of cancer is imminent, but the public re-
     mains skeptical.
imminence *n.,* imminently *adv.*

im-mu-ta-ble *adj.*   *Pronunciation:* ĭm-mū′tă-bl
  Meaning: unchangeable, invariable
  Derivation: Latin *immutabilis,* unchanging
  Examples:
     The laws of nature are immutable and mysterious.
     Some of these adaptations are immutable, but
     others are variable.
immutability and immutableness *n.,* immutably *adv.*

im-pal-pa-ble *adj.*   *Pronunciation:* ĭm-păl′pŭ-bl
  Meaning: intangible, incapable of being perceived by
             the mind or by the senses
  Derivation: Latin *impalpābilis,* untouchable
  Examples:
     The book contained scenes of impalpable beauty.
     An impalpable excitement gripped the audience.
impalpability *n.,* impalpably *adv.*

im-pec-ca-ble *adj.*   *Pronunciation:*   ĭm-pĕk′ŭ-bl
 Meaning: free from fault, blemish, sin, or error
Derivation: Late Latin *impeccābilis,* not liable to sin
Examples:

His taste was impeccable in clothes, if not in the
friends he chose to keep.

Anne's virtually impeccable scholastic record won
her admission to medical school.

impeccability *n.,* impeccably *adv.*

im-pe-cu-ni-ous *adj.*   *Pronunciation:*   ĭm-pĕ-kū′ne-ŭs
 Meaning: without money, poor, destitute
Derivation: French *impécunieux,* poor
Examples:

They originally were a group of impecunious camp
followers, but in time they managed to acquire suf-
ficient means to establish themselves as shopkeep-
ers.

The man turned out to be nothing more than an
impecunious lawyer, able to find clients only
among those even less fortunate than himself.

impecuniousness and impecuniosity *n.,* impecuniously
adv.

im-pede *v.t.*   *Pronunciation:*   ĭm-pēd′
 Meaning: to stop in progress, hinder, obstruct
Derivation: Latin *impedīre,* to entangle the feet

Examples:

> Their journey was impeded for hours by the swamp and the fog.

> You may attempt to impede progress, but you will inevitably fail.

impedance and impeder *n.*, impedingly *adv.*

im-per-cep-ti-ble *adj.*   *Pronunciation:*   ĭm-pēr-sĕp′tĭ-bl

  Meaning: not perceivable by the senses or by the mind; subtle; very slight, insignificant

Derivation: French *imperceptible,* not perceivable

  Examples:

> Dawn was imperceptible, owing to the dense fog over the city.

> The change in his habits, if there was one, was imperceptible to the naked eye.

imperceptibility and imperceptibleness *n.*, imperceptibly *adv.*

im-per-ti-nent *adj.*   *Pronunciation:*   ĭm-pŭr′tĭ-nĕnt

  Meaning: not pertinent, irrelevant, inapplicable; lacking in respect for others; rudely officious, insolent

Derivation: Latin *impertinens,* not belonging

  Examples:

> The argument appeared to him impertinent, not related to the point of his remarks.

> Everyone, including all her classmates, found her impertinent behavior insufferable.

impertinence and impertinency *n.*, impertinently *adv.*

im-pet-u-ous *adj.*   *Pronunciation:*   ĭm-pĕt'ū-ŭs

   Meaning: furious; hastily or rashly energetic; acting with sudden energy; precipitous; rash, impulsive

Derivation: French *impétueux,* impulsive

Examples:

This kind of impetuous behavior should be reserved for some sporting event.

She was one of the most impetuous persons I have ever met.

impetuousness *n.*, impetuously *adv.*

im-plic-it *adj.*   *Pronunciation:*   ĭm-plĭs'ĭt

   Meaning: implied; involved in the nature or being of something, though not shown; unreserved, unquestioning

Derivation: French *implicite,* inherent

Examples:

The football coach demanded implicit obedience from all his players.

They had an implicit understanding that if anything went wrong all would accept the blame and the punishment.

implicitness *n.*, implicitly *adv.*

im-por-tune *v.t.*   *Pronunciation:*   ĭm-pôr-tūn'

   Meaning: to ply or press with requests; to urge persistently; to harass with urgent demands

Derivation: Latin *importūnus,* unfit, troublesome

Examples:

He will not ask for pity, nor will he importune: nothing can be further from his nature.

The man was too honest to bribe and too proud to importune—the situation for the family was hopeless.

importunity and importunateness *n.*, importunate *adj.*, importunely and importunately *adv.*

im-preg-na-ble *adj.*   *Pronunciation:*   ĭm-prĕg′nŭ-bl

   Meaning: strong enough not to be taken by assault; able to resist attack

Derivation: Old French *imprenable,* not takeable

  Examples:

The fort was constructed so that it was impregnable from sea and land.

The logic of his argument made his position impregnable.

impregnability *n.*, impregnably *adv.*

im-pu-dent *adj.*   *Pronunciation:*   ĭm′pū-dĕnt

   Meaning: bold, contemptuous, insolent

Derivation: Latin *impudens,* unashamed

  Examples:

The class was tired of Kate's impudent attitude toward the teacher.

It was the impudence of the person that shocked the group, not his fundamental stand on the problem.

impudence *n.*, impudently *adv.*

in-ane *adj.*   *Pronunciation:* ĭn-ān′
  Meaning: empty, void, vacuous, senseless
  Derivation: Latin *inānis,* empty, vain
  Examples:

> The fool's inane comments embarrassed the hostess, making her wonder why she ever invited him.
> Inanity abounds where stupidity flourishes.

inanity *n.,* inanely *adv.*

in-cho-ate *adj.*   *Pronunciation:* ĭn′kō-ĭt
  Meaning: rudimentary, unfinished, only begun
  Derivation: Latin *inchoare,* to begin
  Examples:

> Inchoate attempts to form a policy plagued the party for the next few months.
> Billions of years ago, life was still in inchoate form, lacking the sophisticated structures commonplace today.

inchoateness *n.,* inchoately *adv.*

in-con-gru-ous *adj.*   *Pronunciation:* ĭn-kŏn′groo-ŭs
  Meaning: not in agreement or harmony; lacking propriety or suitability; illogical
  Derivation: Latin *incongruus,* not in agreement
  Examples:

> Justin uttered such incongruous statements that Jill sometimes feared for his sanity.
> She saw nothing but incongruity in her party's plans and knew they were doomed to failure at the polls.

incongruity and incongruousness *n.,* incongruously *adv.*

in-cred-u-lous *adj.*   *Pronunciation:* ĭn-crĕd'ū-lŭs
  Meaning: skeptical, doubtful, not credible; too ex-
           traordinary to be believed
Derivation: Latin *incrēdere,* not to believe
  Examples:

    The man's snide questions betrayed his incredulous
    attitude.

    We ordinarily dislike incredulity in the young,
    even though we grow increasingly skeptical in old
    age.

incredulity and incredulousness *n.,* incredulously *adv.*

in-dig-e-nous *adj.*   *Pronunciation:* ĭn-dĭj'ĕ-nŭs
  Meaning: occurring naturally in an area or place, na-
           tive; innate
Derivation: Latin *indigenus,* native
  Examples:

    The fish was originally indigenous to South Ameri-
    can waters but now is found throughout the world.

    European business enterprises severely disturbed
    the lives of the indigenous African population.

indigenousness *n.,* indigenously *adv.*

in-dis-cre-tion *n.*   *Pronunciation:* ĭn-dĭs-krĕsh'ŭn
  Meaning: an imprudent, unwise act
Derivation: Latin *in,* not + *discernere,* to distinguish

Examples:
>How many serious indiscretions can a wife forgive?
>I consider those lapses in behavior nothing more than indiscretions, better overlooked than worried over.

indiscreetness *n.*, indiscreet *adj.*, indiscreetly *adv.*

in-e-luc-ta-ble *adj.*   *Pronunciation:* ĭn-ĕ-lŭk′tĭ-bl
 Meaning: irresistible, inevitable; not to be overcome
Derivation: Latin *in,* not + *ēluctābilis,* to be surmounted
 Examples:
>The somber painting recreates the ineluctable process of history.
>Glaciers move onward ineluctably but imperceptibly.

ineluctability *n.*, ineluctably *adv.*

in-ex-o-ra-ble *adj.*   *Pronunciation:* ĭn-ĕk′sō-rŭ-bl
 Meaning: inflexible, relentless, incapable of persuasion
Derivation: Latin *inexōrābilis,* not movable
 Examples:
>The inexorable reality is that the longer the danger exists, the more certain is it that the danger will spread.
>He felt himself pursued inexorably by forces he could not identify.

inexorability and inexorableness *n.*, inexorably *adj.*

in-ex-pli-ca-ble *adj.*   *Pronunciation:* ĭn-ĕks′plĭ-kŭ-bl
   Meaning: incapable of being explained
   Derivation: Latin *inexplicābilis,* that cannot be un-
        folded
   Examples:
      The inexplicable noise in the engine disturbed the
      mechanic, who thought he had performed a com-
      plete overhaul.
      The readers of Gothic novels enjoy characters who
      behave inexplicably.
inexplicability and inexplicableness *n.,* inexplicably *adv.*

in-fat-u-ate *v.t.*   *Pronunciation:* ĭn-făt′ū-āt
   Meaning: to arouse foolish passion; to inspire with
        passion too obstinate to be controlled by
        reason
   Derivation: Latin *infatuatus,* made foolish
   Examples:
      We despise a speaker who is infatuated with the
      sound of his own voice.
      He had an unfortunate tendency to become in-
      fatuated with every woman he met.
infatuation *n.*

in-flex-i-ble *adj.*   *Pronunciation:* ĭn-flĕk′sĭ-bl
   Meaning: rigid, firm, unable to bend or be bent
   Derivation: Latin *inflexibilis,* rigid
   Examples:
      An inflexible attitude in minor matters does not
      win friends.

Happily, she was able to overcome her employees' inflexibility and increase productivity.

inflexibility and inflexibleness *n.*, inflexibly *adv.*

in-gen-i-ous *adj.*   *Pronunciation:* ĭn-jēn′yŭs
  Meaning: inventive, clever
Derivation: Latin *ingeniōsus,* of good natural talent
  Examples:

Her ingenious explanations amazed her mother.

American ingenuity seems to have disappeared in recent years, and the Japanese may now speak of their own inventiveness.

ingenuity and ingeniousness *n.*, ingeniously *adv.*

in-gen-u-ous *adj.*   *Pronunciation:* ĭn-jĕn′ū-ŭs
  Meaning: open, candid, frank, naive, childlike
Derivation: Latin *ingenuus,* freeborn
  Examples:

We expect ingenuous behavior in the young but not in the supposedly mature.

She was no longer young enough to play the ingénue.

ingénue and ingenuousness *n.*, ingenuously *adv.*

in-grained *adj.*   *Pronunciation:* ĭn-grānd′
  Meaning: deep-seated, permeated, inherent
Derivation: Latin *in,* in + *granum,* grain or seed

Examples:

> After a lifetime of scholarship, she exhibits an ingrained insistence on proof before changing an intellectual position.

> Ingrained respect for one's elders characterizes the Chinese family.

ingrain *v.t.*

in-gra-ti-ate *v.t.*   *Pronunciation:* ĭn-grā′shĭ-āt
  Meaning: to work oneself into someone's favor
Derivation: Latin *in,* in + *gratia,* favor
  Examples:

> Try as the student would, he could not ingratiate himself with his English teacher.

> His ingratiating manner was heartily disliked by the older men in the union.

ingratiation *n.,* ingratiating *adj.,* ingratiatingly *adv.*

in-her-ent *adj.*   *Pronunciation:* ĭn-hēr′ĕnt
  Meaning: existing in and inseparable from something else, innate, natural, intrinsic
Derivation: Latin *inhaerens,* sticking to
  Examples:

> The right to govern is inherent in the Faculty Bylaws.

> Inherent honesty is Jane's strongest attribute, but she has much more to recommend her.

inherence *n.,* inhere *v.i.,* inherently *adv.*

in-iq-ui-tous *adj.*   *Pronunciation:*   ĭ-nĭk′wĭ-tŭs
   Meaning: wicked, unjust
   Derivation: Latin *inīquitas,* injustice
   Examples:
      Some of her last remarks were uncharacteristically
      iniquitous and were taken by her friends as a sign of
      declining awareness.
      Even if they have these iniquitous feelings, they
      should keep them to themselves.
   iniquitousness and iniquity *n.,* iniquitously *adv.*

in-nate *adj.*   *Pronunciation:*   ĭn′nāt
   Meaning: inborn, natural
   Derivation: Latin *innātus,* inborn
   Examples:
      An innate grace marked her every action and de-
      lighted all who watched.
      His innate cleverness proved his undoing in busi-
      ness life.
   innateness *n.,* innately *adv.*

in-noc-u-ous *adj.*   *Pronunciation:*   ĭ-nŏk′ū-ŭs
   Meaning: harmless, having no injurious qualities
   Derivation: Latin *innocuus,* not harmful
   Examples:
      If the bomb were as innocuous as claimed, why
      explode it so far from home?
      No one claimed that atomic energy is completely
      innocuous.
   innocuousness *n.,* innocuously *adv.*

in-or-di-nate *adj.*   *Pronunciation:* ĭn-ôr′dĭ-nĭt
  Meaning: excessive, unrestrained, not kept within
               reasonable limits
Derivation: Latin *inordinātus,* disordered
  Examples:
       Disaster can result from inordinate optimism.
       The child's inordinate curiosity meant continual
       trouble for his family.
inordinateness *n.,* inordinately *adv.*

in-scru-ta-ble *adj.*   *Pronunciation:* ĭn-skroo′tŭ-bl
  Meaning: incapable of being understood, incom-
               prehensible, unfathomable
Derivation: Late Latin *inscrūtābilis,* unexamined
  Examples:
       I found his lectures as inscrutable as his facial ex-
       pression.
       Most of the characters in that inscrutable movie
       baffled me, but I was intrigued by the color photog-
       raphy.
inscrutability and inscrutableness *n.,* inscrutably *adv.*

in-sid-i-ous *adj.*   *Pronunciation:* ĭn-sĭd′ĭ-ŭs
  Meaning: wily, treacherous; of hidden harmfulness
Derivation: Latin *insidiōsus,* cunning
  Examples:
       Their insidious actions during the deliberations
       went unnoticed by some of us.

The tumor was the direct result of years of insidious neglect.

insidiousness *n.,* insidiously *adv.*

in-sou-ci-ant *adj.*   *Pronunciation:* ĭn-soo'sĭ-ănt,
                                                 ahn' soo-syähnt
Meaning: indifferent, unconcerned, heedless
Derivation: French *insouciant,* careless
Examples:
His attitude can be described charitably as insouciant.

Dawn's insouciance was part of her charm.

insouciance *n.,* insouciantly *adv.*

in-ter-po-late *v.t.*   *Pronunciation:* ĭn-tŭr' pō-lāt
Meaning: to alter a text or discussion by inserting new
              information or ideas within it
Derivation: Latin *inter,* between + *polire,* to polish
Examples:
She interpolated an acid comment that diverted everyone just when the dean thought he had convinced the faculty.

Senator Percy managed to have his interpolations inserted in the Congressional Record.

interpolation *n.,* interpolative *adj.*

in-tran-si-gent *adj.*   *Pronunciation:* ĭn-trăn'sĭ-jĕnt
Meaning: uncompromising, refusing to accommodate
              another opinion

Derivation: Latin *in,* not + *transigere,* to agree
Examples:

The city fathers were intransigent in their opposition to the proposed real estate reassessment.

Other reasons exist for the intransigent opposition to the oil industry's construction of the pipeline.

intransigence and intransigency *n.,* intransigently *adv.*

in-trep-id *adj.*   *Pronunciation:*   ĭn-trĕp′ĭd
Meaning: fearless, bold
Derivation: Latin *intrepidus,* not alarmed
Examples:

Their intrepid voyage proved that man could survive away from earth.

Joan was so intrepid that others followed her leadership.

intrepidity *n.,* intrepidly *adv.*

in-vei-gle *v.t.*   *Pronunciation:*   ĭn-vē′gl
Meaning: to lead astray by obscuring the proper course; decoy; cajole; entice into action against one's better judgment

Derivation: French *aveugler,* to blind
Examples:

Harriet was inveigled into doing it, although she knew better.

She used her allure in a fruitless attempt to inveigle the physician into performing a hopeless operation.

inveiglement and inveigler *n.*

in-vet-er-ate *adj.*   *Pronunciation:* ĭn-vĕt'ĕr-ĭt
  Meaning: long established, firmly fixed, deep-rooted,
           obstinate
  Derivation: Latin *inveterātus,* made old
  Examples:
    They had an inveterate hatred of one another that
    was difficult for others to understand.
    This unreasonable and inveterate attitude will
    only intensify the problem.
inveterateness *n.,* inveterately *adv.*

in-vid-i-ous *adj.*   *Pronunciation:* ĭn-vĭd'ĭ-ŭs
  Meaning: tending to create ill will or envy, likely to
           give offense
  Derivation: Latin *invidiōsus,* envious
  Examples:
    He slandered her with the most invidious remarks I
    have ever heard.
    The officer remarked that invidious actions like
    that would likely prevent promotion.
invidiousness *n.,* invidiously *adv.*

i-ron-ic *adj.*   *Pronunciation:* ī-rŏn'ĭk
  Meaning: characterized by mocking humor or ridicule
  Derivation: Latin *īronicus,* deceiving

Examples:

> Jane's ironic wit disturbed her sister, who was either too kind or too timid to respond as she should have.

> Many of de Maupassant's stories end in an ironic, almost cruel turn of fate.

irony *n.,* ironical *adj.,* ironically *adv.*

j J j

jeop-ard-y *n.*   *Pronunciation:* jĕp′ērd-ē
  Meaning: exposure to death, injury, or loss; danger
Derivation: French *jeu parti,* an even game
  Examples:

> The detective was in jeopardy because he had failed to lock the criminal in the car.
> English law protects an accused person against double jeopardy.

jeopardize *v.t.*

ju-bi-lant *adj.*   *Pronunciation:* jōō'bĭ'länt
  Meaning: shouting with joy, exulting
  Derivation: Latin *jubilans,* exulting
  Examples:
    The class was jubilant when it learned that the
    term paper was not due for a week.
    The jubilance of the city was unrestrained when its
    team won the World Series.
jubilance *n.*, jubilantly *adv.*

ju-di-cious *adj.*   *Pronunciation:* jū-dĭsh'ŭs
  Meaning: sagacious, discerning, prudent, done with
         reason
  Derivation: French *judicieux* from Latin *jūdicium,*
         judgment
  Examples:
    He was always judicious in his approach to a prob-
    lem.
    The Dean spoke to her in a most judicious manner
    and calmed her quickly.
judiciousness *n.*, judiciously *adv.*

jux-ta-pose *v.t.*   *Pronunciation:* jŭks-tŭ-pōz'
  Meaning: to place side by side
  Derivation: Latin *juxta,* by the side of, near + *positio,*
         placing
  Examples:
    The tapes should not have been so glaringly jux-
    taposed with the secret transcript.

The transcriber mistakenly juxtaposed two words and altered the meaning.

juxtaposition *n.*

k K K k

kin-dred *adj.*   *Pronunciation:* kĭn′drĕd

Meaning: related by origin or qualities; related by
             birth

Derivation: Middle English *kinrede,* related

Examples:
       French, Spanish, and Italian are kindred lan-
       guages.

       Abelard recognized in Eloise a kindred spirit.

kindred *n.*

klep-to-ma-ni-a *n.*   *Pronunciation:* klĕp-tō-mā′nyŭ
  Meaning: neurotic impulse to steal
Derivation: Greek *kleptēs,* thief + *mania,* madness
  Examples:

Kleptomania is a condition that is far more common than we once thought.

Many shoplifters are kleptomaniacs and must receive psychological treatment.

kleptomaniac *n.*

1 L 1

la·con·ic *adj.*   *Pronunciation:* lă-cŏn′ĭk
  Meaning: terseness of speech, sparing of words
Derivation: Latin *lacōnicus,* Spartan
  Examples:

    The detective's laconic manner did not deceive the
    suspect.

    The speaker expressed himself so laconically that
    the speech was over before half the audience was
    seated.

laconically *adv.*

las-civ-i-ous *adj.*   *Pronunciation:* lă-sĭv′ĭ-ŭs
   Meaning: wanton, lewd, lustful
Derivation: Late Latin *lasciviōsus,* wantonness
Examples:
      The dance was so lascivious that the management
      canceled the act for fear of the authorities.
      His lasciviousness repelled his classmates and
      companions.
lasciviousness *n.,* lasciviously *adv.*

las-si-tude *n.*   *Pronunciation:* lăs′sĭ-tūd
   Meaning: faintness, weakness, weariness
Derivation: Latin *lassitūdo,* faintness, weariness
Examples:
      Lassitude for him was ingrained, not acquired.
      The lassitude of the class resulted in lower grades
      and incomplete assignments.

le-thar-gic *adj.*   *Pronunciation:* lĕ-thär′jĭk
   Meaning: sluggish, indifferent, apathetic
Derivation: Late Latin *lēthargia,* sluggishness
Examples:
      The whole group was lethargic because of the late-
      ness of the hour.
      Lethargy was not a common characteristic in a
      steel mill during World War II.
lethargy *n.,* lethargically *adv.*

lo-qua-cious *adj.*   *Pronunciation:* lō-kwā′shŭs
  Meaning: talkative, chatty
Derivation: Latin *loqui,* to talk
  Examples:

> The lawyer's loquacious summation appalled the defendant, who could see the flagging attention of the jury.

> The instructor said that loquaciousness was a virtue only when most of what was said had meaning.

loquaciousness and loquacity *n.*, loquaciously *adv.*

lu-cid *adj.*   *Pronunciation:* lū′sĭd
  Meaning: shining, bright, clear; intellectually bright
Derivation: Latin *lūcidus,* shining
  Examples:

> The professor's lucid explanation impressed the class, which finally understood the point the text had obscured.

> William made the point with admirable lucidity that the Government must support the arts.

lucidity and lucidness *n.*, lucidly *adv.*

lu-di-crous *adj.*   *Pronunciation:* lū′dĭ-krŭs
  Meaning: comical, apt to incite laughter, laughable
Derivation: Latin *lūdicrus,* sportive
  Examples:

> Susan's ludicrous behavior made the entire assembly laugh, so her act was a great success.

Although Sam attempted to appear sophisticated, he succeeded only in appearing ludicrous.

ludicrousness *n.*, ludicrously *adv.*

lu-gu-bri-ous *adj.*   *Pronunciation:* l͞oo-gū′ brĭ-ŭs
  Meaning: mournful, dismal, funereal
  Derivation: Latin *lugubris,* mournful
  Examples:

It was John's opinion that most of his classmates walked around the campus with lugubrious expressions on their faces because they were worried about final examinations.

The assembly witnessed in silence the lugubrious clowning of the class wit.

lugubriousness *n.*, lugubriously *adv.*

lu-mi-nous *adj.*   *Pronunciation:* lū′mĭ-nŭs
  Meaning: shining, emitting light, brilliant, full of light
  Derivation: French *lumineux,* light
  Examples:

His eyes were pale, luminous beacons, seeking a friendly face in a hostile city.

The full moon made the entire beach appear luminous as each wave reflected its light.

luminousness and luminosity *n.*, luminously *adv.*

lu-rid *adj.*   *Pronunciation:* lū′rĭd
  Meaning: harshly vivid or terrible, marked by violent passion or crime

Derivation: Latin *lūridus,* pale yellow
  Examples:
    The critic attacked the book as being too lurid for its
    intended audience.
    She sat in the middle of the room and told one lurid
    story after another.
luridness *n.,* luridly *adv.*

lus-trous *adj.*   *Pronunciation:*   lŭs'trŭs
  Meaning: shining, radiant, having sheen or gloss
Derivation: Old French *lustreux,* shining
  Examples:
    She made a lovely dress out of the lustrous mate-
    rial.
    Jean's eyes were as pale and lustrous as a pearl.
lustrousness *n.,* lustrously *adv.*

m M m

ma-ca-bre *adj.*   *Pronunciation:*   mă-kä′br
  Meaning: gruesome, ghastly, weird
 Derivation: French *macabre,* gruesome
  Examples:

When she had dressed for the role, she had a
macabre appearance that chilled the audience.

For a while, he read only macabre stories, wanting
nothing more than to be frightened by what he
read.

mag-nan-i-mous *adj.*   *Pronunciation:*   măg-năn′ĭ-mŭs
  Meaning: unselfish, high-minded, elevated in soul
Derivation: Latin *magnus,* great + *anima,* soul
  Examples:
    Karla was magnanimous in her treatment of others
    and so was loved by them all.
    Magnanimity is a virtue that is as rare as complete
    honesty.
magnanimity and magnanimousness *n.,* magnani-
mously *adv.*

mal-a-droit *adj.*   *Pronunciation:*   măl-ŭ-droit′
  Meaning: clumsy, awkward, ungainly, lacking in dex-
        terity
Derivation: French *mal,* bad + *à droit,* rightly
  Examples:
    The timing of the news release was singularly
    maladroit.
    She was so maladroit that it was painful to watch
    her attempt any sport.
maladroitness *n.,* maladroitly *adv.*

mal-con-tent *adj.*   *Pronunciation:*   măl′kŭn-tĕnt
  Meaning: discontented, dissatisfied, inclined to rebel
Derivation: Latin *male,* badly + *contentus,* satisfied
  Examples:
    Malcontented students are loudest in their com-
    plaints.
    You will find some malcontents in every institu-
    tion.
malcontent *n.*

ma-lev-o-lent *adj.* *Pronunciation:* mă-lĕv'ō-lĕnt
  Meaning: wishing evil, ill-disposed toward others
  Derivation: Latin *malevolens,* ill-disposed
  Examples:
    Because of their malevolent nature, they repulsed
    all offers of kindness.
    Being raised in city environments can make any-
    one malevolent.
  malevolence *n.,* malevolently *adv.*

ma-li-cious *adj.* *Pronunciation:* mă-lĭsh'ŭs
  Meaning: spiteful, ill-disposed, malevolent
  Derivation: Latin *malus,* bad
  Examples:
    Such a malicious lie should never have been al-
    lowed to appear in print.
    The act seemed at best a malicious jest, at worst an
    outright slander.
  malice and maliciousness *n.,* maliciously *adv.*

ma-lig-nant *adj.* *Pronunciation:* mă-lĭg'nănt
  Meaning: characterized by intense desire to harm;
          harboring ill will or animosity
  Derivation: Latin *malignans,* injuring purposely
  Examples:
    No one could stand the malignant nature that un-
    derlay his insincere friendship.
    If I didn't know better, I would think that malig-
    nant feelings ran in his family.
  malignance and malignancy *n.,* malignantly *adv.*

ma-nip-u-late *v.t.*   *Pronunciation:* mă-nĭp'ū-lāt
  Meaning: to treat or operate with the hands; to man-
               age with the intellect; to manage artfully or
               fraudulently
  Derivation: Latin *manipulus,* handful
  Examples:
        She manipulated the keys of the piano with ease.
        We can sometimes manipulate the law to ease the
        burden on the consumer.
        Kate has learned to manipulate her friends in order
        to get her own way.
manipulation and manipulator *n.,* manipulative and
manipulatory *adj.*

maud-lin *adj.*   *Pronunciation:* môd'lĭn
  Meaning: foolish, overly sentimental, foolishly emo-
               tional
  Derivation: from the proper name *Mary Magdalene*
  Examples:
        They were, perhaps, the most maudlin couple we
        ever encountered, bursting into tears at the
        slightest opportunity.
        I like being sentimental, but I detest being maud-
        lin.

men-da-cious *adj.*   *Pronunciation:* mĕn-dā'shŭs
  Meaning: lying, deceiving, misleading, false, untruth-
               ful
  Derivation: Latin *mendax,* lying, false

Examples:

> It emerged after some discussion that she was not a mendacious person; everything she said was completely true.
>
> If you wish, said the dean, you can accuse him of mendacity, but you had better have firm evidence.

mendacity and mendaciousness *n.*, mendaciously *adv.*

mel-io-rate *v.t., v.i.*   *Pronunciation:* mēl′yō-rāt

  Meaning: *v.t. to make better; v.i.* to become more tolerable

  Derivation: Late Latin *meliorātus,* past part. of *meliōrāre,* to improve

  Examples:

> *v.t.* We hope to meliorate the effects of the strike by increasing our inventory.
>
> *v.i.* What the judge wanted more than anything was to meliorate the sentence if it was at all possible.

melioration *n.*, meliorative *adj.*

mel-lif-lu-ous *adj.*   *Pronunciation:* měl-lĭf′loo-us

  Meaning: flowing smoothly, smooth

  Derivation: Late Latin *mellifluus,* flowing with honey

  Examples:

> She certainly possessed a mellifluous voice.
>
> He could not imagine what the chef had added to the sauce to create such a mellifluous bath for the succulent beef.

mellifluousness *n.*, mellifluously *adv.*

mer-e-tri-cious *adj.*   *Pronunciation:*   mĕr′ ŭ-trĭsh′ ŭs
  Meaning: alluring by false show, flashy, gaudy
Derivation: Latin *meretrīx,* a harlot
  Examples:
    That is the most meretricious deed I have ever
    observed; why can't you behave decently?
    She might have succeeded earlier if she had been
    willing to appear in meretricious roles.
meretriciousness *n.,* meretriciously *adv.*

mer-i-to-ri-ous *adj.*   *Pronunciation:*   mĕr-ĭ-tô′rĭ-ŭs
  Meaning: worthy of reward, gratitude, honor, esteem
Derivation: Latin *meritōrious,* serving to bring in
              money
  Examples:
    His rescue of the drowning child was one of the most
    meritorious acts we ever witnessed.
    Warren made up for his inexperience by his
    meritorious behavior, which earned him the
    gratitude of the entire company.
meritoriousness *n.,* meritoriously *adv.*

me-tic-u-lous *adj.*   *Pronunciation:*   mĕ-tĭk′ū-lŭs
  Meaning: unduly or excessively careful of small de-
              tails, extremely careful
Derivation: Latin *meticulōsus,* fearful
  Examples:
    She was extremely meticulous in her dress and
    spent hours dressing for a party.

All the evidence was meticuously collected by the District Attorney.

meticulosity *n.*, meticulously *adv.*

mi-lieu *n.*   *Pronunciation:*   mē-lyŭ′
  Meaning: environment, setting
Derivation: French *milieu* from Latin *medius*, middle +
              locus, place
  Examples:

She did not care for that milieu at all and longed for home.

The producer was searching for some milieu that would make the main plot more understandable and believable.

mi-nus-cule *adj.*   *Pronunciation:*   mĭ-nŭs′kūl
  Meaning: very small
Derivation: Latin *minusculus*, rather small
  Examples:

The portions served in that restaurant are minuscule, and the diners leave as hungry as when they arrive.

The exhibit was a minuscule version of the entire exposition.

He wrote in a minuscule hand.

minuscule *n.*, minuscular *adj.*

mit-i-gate *v.t., v.i.*   *Pronunciation:*   mĭt′ĭ-gāt
  Meaning: to make or become less severe, harsh; to
            meliorate

Derivation: Latin *mītigātus,* past part. of *mītigāre,* to
                soften
Examples:
        Throat irritation is mitigated somewhat by swal-
        lowing cream.
        I wanted at all costs to mitigate the effects of the
        strike at the plant.
mitigation *n.,* mitigative and mitigatory *adj.*

mol-li-fy *v.t.*   *Pronunciation:*   mŏl'ĭ-fī
    Meaning: to appease rage; to allay, mitigate
Derivation: Latin *mollificāre,* to soften
Examples:
        She tried to mollify him but didn't succeed.
        Her ability to mollify angry customers won the
        approval of her superiors.
mollification *n.,* mollifiable *adj.*

mo-rass *n.*   *Pronunciation:*   mŭ-răs'
    Meaning: a marsh, swamp
Derivation: Dutch *moeras,* marsh
Examples:
        We seemed to have been in this morass for days.
        In spite of all our efforts, our debts formed an im-
        penetrable morass into which we were slowly sink-
        ing.

mor-bid *adj.*   *Pronunciation:*   môr'bĭd
    Meaning: impressed by ideas of a gloomy sort, grue-
                some

Derivation: Latin *morbidus,* sickly
Examples:

> Howard's morbid nature seemed inherited—his entire family never showed any sign of happiness.
>
> Morbidity can approach a pathological condition if one is not careful.

morbidity and morbidness *n.,* morbidly *adv.*

mor-i-bund *adj.*   *Pronunciation:*   môr′ĭ-bŭnd
   Meaning: in a dying state, near death
Derivation: Latin *moribundus,* dying
Examples:

> When the doctor arrived, the patient seemed moribund.
>
> She specialized in bringing moribund businesses back to a profitable condition.

moribundity *n.,* moribundly *adv.*

my-o-pi-a *n.*   *Pronunciation:*   mī-ō′pĭ-ă
   Meaning: shortsightedness
Derivation: Greek *myōps,* shortsighted
Examples:

> The teacher's myopia got worse as the semester progressed.
>
> He was so myopic about his future that he could not look beyond the next day.

myopic *adj.*

n N n

neb-u-lous *adj.*   *Pronunciation:*   nĕb′ū-lŭs

  Meaning: hazy, vague; cloudy, misty

Derivation: Latin *nebulosus,* cloudy

  Examples:

> He supplied several nebulous answers that satis
> fied no one and then left.

> Her nebulous ideas could never be formulated
> coherently.

nebulousness *n.,* nebulously *adv.*

ne-far-i-ous *adj.*   *Pronunciation:* nĕ-fär′ĭ-ŭs
  Meaning: wicked, iniquitous
  Derivation: Latin *nefārius,* impious
  Examples:
    His nefarious schemes almost always fail, but he
    cannot bring himself to undertake honest work.
    That was a most nefarious crime, and I hope the
    police will be able to find its perpetrator.
nefariousness *n.,* nefariously *adv.*

nem-e-sis *n.*   *Pronunciation:* nĕm′ĕ-sĭs
  Meaning: one who or something that inflicts retribu-
        tion; bane, curse
  Derivation: Greek *Nemesis,* goddess of retribution
  Examples:
    She seemed to have been his nemesis since the day
    they met.
    Her nemesis lay in wait behind the white door of the
    refrigerator: peanut butter and jelly.

nig-gard *n.*   *Pronunciation:* nĭg′ērd
  Meaning: a miser, one very stingy with money
  Derivation: Middle English *nigard,* miser
  Examples:
    He was forced to work for such low pay because he
    needed the work and his employer was a niggard.
    Since he was poor and out of work, he was willing to
    accept a job at niggardly pay until a better one came
    along.
niggardliness *n.,* niggardly *adj.*

non-de-script *adj.*   *Pronunciation:* nŏn′dĕ-skrĭpt
   Meaning: not belonging to any particular class or kind
Derivation: Latin *non,* not + *dēscriptus,* described
Examples:

   She hung around with the most nondescript charac-
   ter I have ever seen.

   The dress was one of those nondescript things you
   think are bargains, the time you buy them.

nondescriptly *adv.*

nu-ance *n.*   *Pronunciation:*   nū-äns′
   Meaning: shade of difference, subtle gradation, deli-
                cate variation
Derivation: Old French *muance,* variation + *nue,* cloud
Examples:

   His prose style contained nuances I had never encountered before in the work of one so young.

   The lecturer explained every nuance in the story,
   boring some of his audience but enriching those
   who were attentive.

o O o

ob-fus-cate *v.t.*   *Pronunciation:*   ŏb-fŭs'kāt

  Meaning: confuse, bewilder, obscure

Derivation: Latin *obfuscātus,* past part. of *obfuscāre,* to
            darken

  Examples:

> The issue was obfuscated by several politicians
> seeking vainly to clarify it.
>
> The instructor thought he had provided a solution,
> but the class thought he had obfuscated the prob-
> lem.

obfuscation *n.*

ob-nox-ious *adj.*   *Pronunciation:*   ŏb-nŏk′shŭs
  Meaning: offensive, objectionable
Derivation: Latin *obnoxius,* exposed to harm
  Examples:

> He is the most obnoxious person I have ever known,
> but I cannot tell you why.
>
> She couldn't understand why Hollywood produced
> so many obnoxious pictures.

obnoxiousness *n.,* obnoxiously *adv.*

ob-se-qui-ous *adj.*   *Pronunciation:*   ŏb-sē-kwĭ-ŭs
  Meaning: servile, overly attentive, currying favor
Derivation: Latin *obsequiōsus,* compliant
  Examples:

> His obsequious manner offended everyone, even
> though he intended no harm.
>
> It never entered her mind to perform so obsequious
> an act, but the situation seemed to call for it.

obsequiousness *n.,* obsequiously *adv.*

ob-strep-er-ous *adj.*   *Pronunciation:*   ŏb-strĕp′ĕr-ŭs
  Meaning: vociferous, noisy, tumultuous
Derivation: Latin *obstreperus,* clamorous
  Examples:

> Obstreperous children are often hyperactive and
> must be treated carefully.
>
> The crowd was so obstreperous that the speaker
> could not be heard.

obstreperousness *n.,* obstreperously *adv.*

ob-tuse *adj.*   *Pronunciation:* ŏb-tūs′
  Meaning: dull, blunt, stupid, insensitive, dense, thick-headed
  Derivation: Latin *obtūsus,* dulled
  Examples:
    That novelist's style is so obtuse that most readers cannot understand his books.
    She wondered if he was so obtuse because he had never been with people before.
obtuseness *n.,* obtusely *adv.*

oc-cult *adj., n.*   *Pronunciation:* ŏ-kŭlt′
  Meaning: *adj.* beyond the scope of one's understanding, mysterious; *n.* anything beyond understanding
  Derivation: Latin *occultus,* past part. *occulere,* to cover up, hide
  Examples:
    n. Occult practices are becoming more prevalent.
    adj. Elsa was very interested in anything pertaining to the occult.

om-i-nous *adj.*   *Pronunciation:* ŏm′ĭ-nŭs
  Meaning: portentious, foretelling evil, inauspicious
  Derivation: Latin *ōminōsus,* portentous

Examples:

The first ominous claps of thunder sent all of them home.

These ominous threats of war could endanger world peace.

omen and ominousness *n.*, ominously *adv.*

om-nip-o-tent *adj.*   *Pronunciation:*   ŏm-nĭp′ŭ-tĕnt
  Meaning: all-powerful
Derivation: Latin *omnipotens,* almighty
  Examples:

He was the most feared ruler on earth, believed omnipotent by his subjects.

If I felt as omnipotent as she does, I would run for the presidency.

omnipotence *n.*, omnipotently *adv.*

op-por-tune *adj.*   *Pronunciation:*   ŏp-ôr-tūn′
  Meaning: appropriate, favorable, timely
Derivation: Latin *opportūnus,* driving toward the har-
          bor
  Examples:

She thought it an opportune moment to talk to him about a raise.

The dinner table was the place for an opportune request for additional lunch money.

opportuneness *n.*, opportunely, *adv.*

op-pro-bri-ous *adj.*   *Pronunciation:*   ŭ-prō′brē-ŭs
  Meaning: scurrilous, disgraceful, shameful

Derivation: Latin *opprōbriōsus,* infamous
Examples:

She called him an opprobrious name and left, vowing never to see him again.

Harry's opprobrious behavior was called to the attention of the Academy, but to no avail.

opprobriousness *n.,* opprobriously *adv.*

o-ro-tund *adj.*   *Pronunciation:* ō'rŭ-tŭnd
Meaning: fullness of sound, sonorous
Derivation: Latin *ōre retundō,* with round mouth
Examples:

Politicians, in their orotund fashion, talked of "constitutional crisis," and they were right.

He delivered the address in orotund phrases far better for the ear than for the mind.

os-ten-si-ble *adj.*   *Pronunciation:* ŏs-tĕn'sĭ-bl
Meaning: avowed, apparent, showing outwardly
Derivation: Latin *ostensus,* displayed
Examples:

Her ostensible position on the subject was far from the one she held privately.

One problem was that the people who were ostensibly in charge could not make decisions.

ostensibly *adv.*

os-ten-ta-tious *adj.*   *Pronunciation:* ŏs-tĕn-tā'shŭs
Meaning: fond of self-display, showy, pretentious

Derivation: see *ostensible*
Examples:

Like monkeys in a zoo, many people are given to ostentatious behavior to attract an audience.

Many people were sick of her ostentatious jewelry and clothing.

ostentation *n.*, ostentatiously *adv.*

p P p

par-a-digm *n.*   *Pronunciation:* păr′ă-dĭm, păr′ă-dīm
  Meaning: model, pattern
Derivation: French *paradigme,* example
Examples:

One sociologist sees the sexual behavior of the culture as a paradigm for its general social organization.

She constructed a paradigm for her students to consider.

paradigmatic *adj.*

par-si-mo-ni-ous *adj.*   *Pronunciation:*   pär-sĭ-mō'nĭ-ŭs
  Meaning: frugal, niggardly, stingy
  Derivation: Latin *parsimōnia,* sparingness
  Examples:
    She considered her father parsimonious, but others
    thought of him in even worse terms.
    Parsimony in business, more often than not, is poor
    business.
  parsimony *n.,* parsimoniously *adv.*

pen-chant *n.*   *Pronunciation:*   pĕn'chănt, pän'shän
  Meaning: strong inclination or leaning
  Derivation: French *pencher,* to bend
  Examples:
    Our newspapers have a penchant for oversimplifi-
    cation in order to attract the widest possible reader-
    ship.
    Jones had a penchant for elaborate terminology
    that annoyed his readers.

per-di-tion *n.*   *Pronunciation:*   pŭr-dĭsh'ŭn
  Meaning: final spiritual ruin, hell, utter destruction
  Derivation: Latin *perditio,* act of destroying
  Examples:
    The revivalist preached that the people were pre-
    pared neither for redemption nor perdition.
    Can we stand by in complete safety while others
    risk perdition?

per-emp-tory *adj.*   *Pronunciation:* pŭr-ĕmp'tō-rē
  Meaning: absolute,   conclusive;   incontrovertible,
        positive; arrogant
  Derivation: Latin *peremptorius*, destructive, decisive
  Examples:

   Because the lawyers had already used their right to
   make ten peremptory challenges, several jurors
   were seated who appeared hostile to the defen-
   dants.

   His peremptory behavior made him few friends.

  peremptoriness *n.*, peremptorily *adv.*

per-fi-di-ous *adj.*   *Pronunciation:* pŭr-fĭ'dē-ŭs
  Meaning: faithless, treacherous
  Derivation: Latin *perfidiosus*, faithless
  Examples:

   Major Andre was accused of perfidious acts detri-
   mental to the American revolution.

   What appeared to be perfidious actions turned out
   to be patriotic behavior in the highest sense.

  perfidy and perfidiousness *n.*, perfidiously *adv.*

per-func-tory *adj.*   *Pronunciation:* pŭr-fŭnk'tō-rē
  Meaning: done superficially or carelessly; indifferent
  Derivation: Latin *perfunctus*, discharged

Examples:

They had made only the most perfunctory provisions for moving their furniture, even though the moving van was expected within two hours.

She indicated clearly that her interest in the matter was perfunctory at best.

perfunctoriness *n.*, perfunctorily *adv.*

per-im-e-ter *n.*   *Pronunciation:*   pŭ-rĭm′ĭ-tŭr

Meaning: outer boundary of a geometric figure or a military unit

Derivation: Greek *perimetros,* perimeter

Examples:

There is a simple formula for measuring the perimeter of a circle.

Two squads of infantrymen were assigned the important task of guarding the company's perimeter.

perimetric and perimetrical *adj.*, perimetrically *adv.*

pe-riph-er-al *adj.*   *Pronunciation:*   pŭ-rĭf′ŭr-ŭl

Meaning: away from the central area of interest, external

Derivation: Greek *periphérein,* to carry

Examples:

My interest in the lecturer's topic was only peripheral, so I soon left to study in the library.

Peripheral issues in the campaign were ignored by the voters, who could think only of the problems of jobs and inflation.

periphery *n.*, peripherally *adv.*

per-me-ate *v.t., v.i.*   *Pronunciation:* pẽr′me-at

  Meaning: *v.t.* to pass through the pores or interstices of; *v.i.* to spread or diffuse

  Derivation: Latin *permeatus,* past part. of *permeare,* to pass through

  Examples:

    v.t. Water had permeated the entire stretch of sand, making it difficult to walk through.

    v.t. A feeling of defeat was so strong that it permeated our daily lives.

    v.i. The smell of cigarette smoke permeated throughout the train car.

permeation *n.,* permeative *adj.*

per-ni-cious *adj.*   *Pronunciation:* pŭr-nĭsh′ŭs

  Meaning: highly destructive and injurious; deadly, evil; wicked, malevolent

  Derivation: Latin *perniciosus,* death by violence

  Examples:

    Vice is a pernicious threat to life in big cities.

    Pernicious anemia is a disease that leaves little hope for the afflicted.

perniciousness *n.,* perniciously *adv.*

per-sist-ent *adj.*   *Pronunciation:* pẽr-sĭst′ĕnt

  Meaning: determined, persevering, continuing steadily in the same direction

  Derivation: Latin *persistere,* to remain steadfast

Examples:

The doctor was persistent in his research for a cure for the common cold.

The boat made headway because the Captain was persistent and skillful.

persistence *n.,* persistently *adv.*

per-tur-ba-tion *n.*   *Pronunciation:*   pûr-tēr-bā′shŭn

Meaning: something disquieting, distressful, or troublesome

Derivation: Latin *perturbāre,* to disturb

Examples:

Changes in our plans have caused perturbations all along the line.

He hoped that his decision would not result in perturbations in the normal routine.

perturb *v.t.,* perturbable *adj.*

pet-u-lant *adj.*   *Pronunciation:*   pĕtch′ū-lĕnt

Meaning: habitually complaining or fretting, ill-humored

Derivation: Latin *petulans,* making slight attacks on

Examples:

The petulant child seriously disturbed his family's routine.

While we may excuse the patient's petulant behavior, we certainly do not welcome it.

We heartily dislike the petulance in most of his prose.

petulance and petulancy *n.,* petulantly *adv.*

phleg-ma-tic *adj.*   *Pronunciation:* flĕg-măt′ĭk
  Meaning: sluggish, hard to arouse to activity
  Derivation: Greek *phlegmatikós,* sluggish
  Examples:
      The physician had no explanation for the phlegma-
      tic attitude of his patient.
      By early winter, some animals begin to reduce their
      activities and soon appear phlegmatic.
  phlegmatically *adv.*

pil-lo-ry *n., v.t.*   *Pronunciation:* pĭl′ŭ-rē
  Meaning: *n.* a frame having holes for the head and
              hands, used for punishment in a public area;
              v.t. to punish severely with or without a pil-
              lory, expose to public scorn
  Derivation: Old French *pilori,* pillory
  Examples:
      n. Modern penal institutions do not use the pillory
      as a means of punishment.
      v.t. Their vicious critical attack pilloried the unfor-
      tunate poet, who never recovered his reputation.

plain-tive *adj.*   *Pronunciation:* plān′tĭv
  Meaning: expressive of sorrow
  Derivation: Old French *plaintif,* complaining
  Examples:
      The child had learned to strike an appropriately
      plaintive note when asking for forgiveness.
      Her voice was almost plaintive as she pleaded her
      client's case before the stern jury.
  plaintiveness *n.,* plaintively *adv.*

poi·gnant *adj.*   *Pronunciation:* poīn'yŭnt
  Meaning: painfully moving, arousing sympathy
Derivation: Old French *poindre,* to sting
  Examples:

Expressions that the actor intended as poignant turned out to be ludicrous.

The bride's farewell to her old grandfather was a poignant moment in an otherwise joyous day.

poignancy *n.,* poignantly *adv.*

po·lem·ic *n., adj.*   *Pronunciation:* pō-lĕm'ĭk
  Meaning: *n.* a controversial argument, one who engages in controversial argument, the art of controversy (when spelled with an *s,* i.e., polemics); *adj.* pertaining to controversy, controversial
Derivation: Greek *polemikos,* warlike
  Examples:

adj. John Milton was a polemicist as well as poet.

n. The committee, growing tired of the chairman's lengthy polemics, rose as one person and left the room.

n. Many great political figures have made their marks by publishing polemic pamphlets on subjects of current interest.

polemicist and polemist *n.,* polemical *adj.,* polemically *adv.*

pomp·ous *adj.*   *Pronunciation:* pŏmp'ŭs
  Meaning: self-important, showy, exhibiting ostentation

Derivation: French *pompeux,* pompous
Examples:
   The dentist, inflated by his financial success, became a pompous bore.
   Pomposity fails to impress anyone with a grain of
   good sense.
pomposity and pompousness *n.,* pompously *adv.*

pon-tif-i-cate *v.i.*   *Pronunciation:*   pŏn-tĭf'ĭ-kāt
   Meaning: to speak pompously
Derivation: Latin *pontifex,* bridge builder
Examples:
   Samuel Johnson would pontificate for hours on end,
   delighting his audience with his wit and putting it
   to sleep with his persistence.
   How can you pontificate on a subject you under-
   stand so poorly?

por-ten-tous *adj.*   *Pronunciation:*   pôr-tĕn'tŭs
   Meaning: ominous, warning of evil
Derivation: Latin *portentum,* forewarning
Examples:
   The portentous rise in the number of unemployed
   caused many of us to become pessimistic.
   Writers of mystery novels employ portentous
   shrieks and cries to chill the reader.
   This failure portends disaster.
portentousness *n.,* portend *v.t.,* portentously *adv.*

pre-cip-i-tous *adj.*   *Pronunciation:*   prĭ-sĭp'ĭ-tŭs
  Meaning: steep, almost vertical, rapidly descending
  Derivation: French *précipiteux,* resembling a precipice
  Examples:

> Following his censure by his colleagues, the Senator encountered hostility among his constituents sufficient to cause his precipitous decline.

> They failed in their attempt to climb the precipitous glacier and barely managed to return safely.

precipice and precipitousness *n.,* precipitate *adj.,* precipitously *adv.*

pre-co-cious *adj.*   *Pronunciation:*   prĕ-kō'shŭs
  Meaning: mentally or physically developed beyond one's years
  Derivation: Latin *praecoquere,* to cook beforehand
  Examples:

> The precocious young girl was already an accomplished violinist, but no one described her as a child prodigy.

> As a boy, John Stuart Mill showed an intellectual precocity that frightened other children.

precocity and precociousness *n.,* precociously *adv.*

pre-con-cept-ion *n. Pronunciation:*   prē-kŭn-sĕp'shŭn
  Meaning: prejudice, opinion held before there is full knowledge of a matter
  Derivation: Latin *praeconcipere,* to preconceive

Examples:

While we cannot help but have preconceptions, we must overcome them if we are to be fair in our final judgment of the affair.

His preconceptions happily proved false, and the evening proved amply entertaining.

preconceive *v.t.*

pred-a-to-ry *adj.* *Pronunciation:* prĕd'ŭh-tō-rē
 Meaning: plundering, pillaging, living by hunting
Derivation: Latin *praedatorius,* hunting
 Examples:

Man is considered the most predatory of all mammals, willing to kill anything and eat most of what he kills.

Business need not be a predatory activity.

predatoriness and predator *n.,* predacious *adj.,* predatorily *adv.*

pre-med-i-tat-ed *adj.* *Pronunciation:* prĭ-mĕd'ĭ-tāt-ĭd
 Meaning: planned or considered beforehand, contrived
Derivation: Latin *praemeditatus,* thought through beforehand
 Examples:

Premeditated murder is legally termed murder in the first degree.

His impertinent remark came so quickly that it could not have been premeditated.

premeditation *n.,* premeditate *v.i.,* premeditative *adj.*

pres·ti·gious *adj.*   *Pronunciation:*   prĕs-tēj′ŭs
   Meaning: arousing admiration, renown, respect
Derivation: Latin *praestīgium,* delusion
   Examples:
      All he wanted was prestigious public office without
      responsibility or power.
      The prestige she gained as a result of her appoint-
      ment did not change her fundamental humility.
prestige *n.*

pre·ten·tious *adj.*   *Pronunciation:*   prē-tĕn′shŭs
   Meaning: overassuming, claiming too much, osten-
               tatious, showy
Derivation: Latin *pretendere,* to stretch
   Examples:
      The publisher made pretentious claims for the
      quality of the book even after reviewers had pointed
      out its faults.
      The new neighbors were accused unjustly of preten-
      tious attitudes.
pretentiousness *n.*, pretentiously *adv.*

pro·cliv·i·ty *n.*   *Pronunciation:*   prō-klĭv′ĭ-tē
   Meaning: natural inclination, innate tendency, lean-
               ing
Derivation: Latin *proclīvitas,* tendency
   Examples:
      Who among us has a proclivity for mirth in a time of
      tragedy?
      The physician told the patient that his proclivity for
      alcohol would ruin his health.

pro-cras-ti-nate *v.i.*   *Pronunciation:* prō-krăs′tĭ-nāt
  Meaning: put off, delay, postpone
Derivation: Latin *prōcrastināre,* put off until tomorrow
Examples:

> He who procrastinates may spend more energy in worrying about missed deadlines than he would in completing his work.

> A reporter for a daily newspaper cannot procrastinate if he is to complete his work on time.

procrastination and procrastinator *n.*

prod-i-gal *n., adj.*   *Pronunciation:* prŏd′ĭ-gl
  Meaning: *n.* spendthrift; *adj.* recklessly extravagant, wastefully lavish
Derivation: Latin *prōdigere,* to squander
Examples:

> *adj.* A young prodigal usually matures as an indigent adult.

> *n.* A prodigal son needs a wealthy father.

prodigality *n.,* prodigally *adv.*

pro-di-gious *adj.*   *Pronunciation:* prō-dĭj′ŭs
  Meaning: marvelous, extraordinary, vast
Derivation: Latin *prōdigiōsus,* ominous
Examples:

> The prodigious oil resources of the Arab countries dwarf the ability of poor nations to pay for their fuel.

> To the annoyance of her husband, her prodigious appetite for well-prepared food overtook her in middle age.

prodigiousness *n.,* prodigiously *adv.*

pro-fi-cient *n.*   *Pronunciation:* prō-fĭsh′ŭnt
   Meaning: knowledgable in any art, science, or branch
                of learning; skillful, adept
   Derivation: Latin *proficiens,* progressing
   Examples:
       She was so proficient in all her studies that she was
       advanced rapidly.
       If you cannot do it proficiently, don't do it at all.
   proficiency *n.,* proficiently *adv.*

pro-found *adj.*   *Pronunciation:* prō-found′
   Meaning: intellectually deep, thorough; coming from a
                depth, deep-seated
   Derivation: Latin *profundus,* bottom
   Examples:
       She spoke with such profound feeling that she con-
       vinced everyone in the audience.
       The contents of the book were so profound that it
       was difficult to read quickly.
   profundity and profoundness *n.,* profoundly *adv.*

pro-fuse *adj.*   *Pronunciation:* prō-fūs′
   Meaning: bountiful, lavish, pouring forth liberally
   Derivation: Latin *profusus,* past part. of *profundere,* to
                pour out
   Examples:
       The portions at this restaurant are profuse without
       being overwhelming, but the quality of the food is
       not very high.

All the critics were profuse in their praise of the play.

profuseness *n.,* profusely *adv.*

prog-no-sis *n.*   *Pronunciation:*   prŏg-nō'sĭs
   Meaning: a forecast of the progress of a disease; a fore-cast
Derivation: Greek *prognōsis,* foreknowledge
Examples:

   The prognosis for many cancers is not good.

   They were very guarded in their discussion of the merger, but they agreed that the prognosis seemed excellent.

prognostication and prognosticator *n.,* prognostic *adj.*

pro-lif-er-ate *v.i.*   *Pronunciation:*   prō-lĭf'ŭr-āt
   Meaning: to grow rapidly by the production of new parts, cells, or buds
Derivation: Latin *prōli,* offspring + *fero,* to bear
Examples:

   The irises proliferated so rapidly that some of the clumps had to be dug out.

   If you allow some less desirable fish to proliferate, you will surely run into trouble at the fish farm.

   Their troubles proliferated.

proliferation *n.,* proliferous *adj.*

pro-lif-ic *adj.*   *Pronunciation:* prō-lĭf′ĭk
  Meaning: fruitful, teeming, fertile, producing abun-
               dantly
  Derivation: Latin *proli,* offsping + *facere,* to make
  Examples:
               She is a very prolific writer, often producing two
               books a year.
               If I were as prolific a painter as you, I wouldn't have
               to worry about money.
prolificness *n.,* prolifically *adv.*

pro-pen-si-ty *n.*   *Pronunciation:* ‚prō-pĕn′sĭ-tē
  Meaning: tendency, predisposition, natural bias,
               proneness
  Derivation: Latin *pro,* forward + *pendere,* to hang
  Examples:
               She had a strong propensity for hard work and long
               hours.
               I believe his propensity for red wines is inherited
               from his father.

pro-pin-qui-ty *n.*   *Pronunciation:* prō-pĭn′kwŭ-tē
  Meaning: nearness of place, time, or blood; kinship
  Derivation: Latin *propinquitas,* nearness
  Examples:
               The propinquity of the suspects at the time of the
               crime effectively prevented the officers from pursu-
               ing any other leads.

After discussing the relationship for a few minutes, they discovered that the degree of propinquity was great enough to suggest a genetic factor in the disease.

pro-pi-ti-ate *v.t.*   *Pronunciation:*   prō-pĭsh'ĭ-āt
 Meaning: to gain the favor of, appease, conciliate
Derivation: Latin *propitiātus,* favorable
Examples:

Every effort was made to propitiate the irate parents but without success.

Although he failed to propitiate the general, there was no doubt that a degree of reasonableness had been achieved.

propitiator *n.,* propitiative and propitiable *adj.*

pro-pi-tious *adj.*   *Pronunciation:*   prō-pĭsh'ŭs
 Meaning: favorably disposed, of good omen, auspicious
Derivation: Latin *propitius,* favorable
Examples:

I don't think this a propitious moment for you to request a change of grade.

She took the eclipse as a propitious sign from the stars and decided to launch her law career.

propitiousness *n.,* propitiously *adv.*

pru-ri-ent *adj.*   *Pronunciation:*   proor'ĭ-ĕnt
 Meaning: having lewd longings or lascivious desires
Derivation: Latin *prūriens* past part. of *prūire,* to itch

Examples:

The prurient nature of the book appealed to some readers, but it repelled others.

What she regarded as prurience, he considered a healthy interest in life.

prurience and pruriency *n.,* pruriently *adv.*

pu-er-ile *adj.*   *Pronunciation:*   pū′ĕr-ĭl

  Meaning: childish, foolish, unthinking

Derivation: Latin *puerīlis* from *puer,* child

  Examples:

Several of John's teachers were critical of his puerile devotion to games and his lack of concern for serious studies.

The instructor maintained that the book was not profound in the least—that the style, diction, and level were all puerile.

puerilely *adv.*

punc-til-i-ous *adj.*   *Pronunciation:*   pŭnk-tĭl′ĭ-ŭs

  Meaning: precise, particular, strict, scrupulously exact in detail, minutely observant of formalities

Derivation: Latin *punctum,* point

  Examples:

The store manager was impressed by his cashier's punctilious habits.

The ceremony was carried out with punctilious attention to the rules of orthodoxy.

punctiliousness *n.,* punctiliously *adv.*

pur-loin *v.t.*   *Pronunciation:*   pẽr-loin′
  Meaning: to steal, appropriate, pilfer, snatch
  Derivation: Old French *purloigner,* to retard, delay
  Examples:

> The thief returned the purloined manuscript to the author when he realized he could not use it in any way.

> He learned after an arduous investigation that the painted scroll had been purloined from the Louvre.

purloiner *n.*

pur-port *n., v.t.*   *Pronunciation:*   *n.* pŭr′pôrt,
                                        v. pŭr-pôrt′
  Meaning: *n.* meaning, substance; *v.t.* to profess, claim
  Derivation: Latin *proportāre,* to carry or bear forth
  Examples:

> *n.* The purport of her remarks was accurately reported in most of the morning newspapers.

> *v.t.* She is purported to have been admitted to a previously all-male college.

pu-sil-lan-i-mous *adj.*   *Pronunciation:*   pū-sĭ-lăn′ĭ-mŭs
  Meaning: cowardly, timid, fearful of danger, faint-hearted
  Derivation: Latin *pusillus,* very little + *animus,* spirit
  Examples:

> The sergeant stated that pusillanimous men had no role in the military.

> She spoke with contempt of his pusillanimous actions.

pusillanimity *n.,* pusillanimously *adv.*

q Q q

qualm *n.*   *Pronunciation:* kwäm

  Meaning: a sudden attack of illness, faintness, or pain;
                a sudden misgiving or faintheartedness

Derivation: Anglo-Saxon *cwealm,* death

Examples:

      Sheila had no qualms about accepting a ride from
      him, since he was a friend of her father's.

      He felt qualmish about the whole situation, be-
      cause he knew everyone they were talking about.

qualmishness *n.,* qualmish *adj.,* qualmishly *adv.*

quan-da-ry *n.*   *Pronunciation:*   kwŏn′dŭ-rē

  Meaning: a state of perplexity or doubt

Derivation: perhaps from Latin *quandō,* when

  Examples:

> The company's executives were in a quandary about whether to diversify or not.

> He suggested that they resolve the quandary by staying home rather than argue over which movie to see.

quer-u-lous *adj.*   *Pronunciation:*   kwĕr′ŭ-lŭs,
                                          kwĕr′yŭ-lŭs

  Meaning: apt to find fault, habitually complaining, fretful, peevish

Derivation: Latin *querulus,* complaining

  Examples:

> The customer was querulous throughout dinner about the service the waiter was giving him.

> I know he is querulous by nature, but that doesn't explain his obnoxious behavior.

querulousness *n.,* querulously *adv.*

qui-es-cent *adj.*   *Pronunciation:*   kwĭ-ĕs′ĕnt

  Meaning: still, calm, dormant, tranquil, serene, placid, at rest, motionless

Derivation: Latin *quiescere,* to keep quiet

Examples:

That volcano has been blessedly quiescent for many months.

Although the physician considered the disease to be quiescent, he saw the patient every month.

quiescence *n.*, quiescently *adv.*

quin-tes-sence *n.*   *Pronunciation:*   kwĭn-tĕs′ĕns
   Meaning: essential element, purest part, the essence of a thing in its purest form
 Derivation: Middle Latin *quinta essentia,* fifth essence
   Examples:

According to Aristotle, quintessence was the substance of the heavenly bodies.

Jean Harlow was quintessential Hollywood in her day.

quintessential *adj.*

r R r

ran-cor *n.*   *Pronunciation:*   răn′kŭr

   Meaning: extreme ill will, deep-seated enmity, persis-
               tent grudge or animosity

Derivation: Latin *rancere,* to be sour

  Examples:

     The instructor believed that the department head
     showed rancor in his dealings with his staff.

     Rancorous debate in the House of Commons de-
     layed passage of the new legislation.

rancorousness *n.,* rancorous *adj.,* rancorously *adv.*

ra-pa-cious *adj.*   *Pronunciation:* ră-pā′shŭs
  Meaning: extremely grasping; inclined to seize that
          which is desired
  Derivation: Latin *rapere,* to seize and carry off
  Examples:

    The rapacious landlord raised his rents as often as
    the law allowed.

    He was known as one of the most rapacious grafters
    in Equope, stopping at nothing to enrich himself.

rapaciousness and rapacity *n.,* rapaciously *adv.*

re-cid-i-vist *n.*   *Pronunciation:* rĕ-sĭd′ĭ-vĭst
  Meaning: one who falls back into earlier undesirable
          habits, especially a criminal who returns to
          criminal life after being released from
          prison
  Derivation: Latin *recidere,* to fall back
  Examples:

    The Fortune Society achieves some measure of suc-
    cess in preventing former prisoners from becoming
    recidivists.

    Most prison systems fail to diminish recidivism be-
    cause they do little to encourage character change
    in their inmates.

recidivism *n.,* recidivistic *adj.*

rec-on-noi-ter *v.t.*   *Pronunciation:* rĕk-ŭ-noi′tŭr
  Meaning: to examine or survey, especially with a
          military or engineering purpose

Derivation: French *reconnoitre,* reconnoiter
Examples:

> The Indian scout was given the task of reconnoitering the area west of the advancing column.
>
> If you reconnoiter the land ahead carefully, you will minimize casualties.

reconnoiterer and reconnaissance *n.*

re-crim-i-na-tion *n. Pronunciation:*   rĕ-krĭm-ĭ-nā′shŭn
Meaning: a countercharge or accusation
Derivation: Middle Latin *recrīmināre,* to accuse again of a crime
Examples:

> The judge ruled that the defense could not express anymore recriminations in court.
>
> Rather than hear any further recriminations from her mother, Sheila left.

recriminate *v.t., v.i.,* recriminatory and recriminative *adj.*

rec-ti-tude *n.*   *Pronunciation:*   rĕk′tĭ-tūd
Meaning: righteousness, goodness, honesty, integrity, probity
Derivation: Latin *rectus,* straight, right
Examples:

> The parson, in praising the action of one of the parishioners, spoke of his rectitude and devotion.
>
> No one could condemn the rectitude with which he approached the problem.

re-cum-bent *adj.*   *Pronunciation:* rē-kŭm'bĕnt
  Meaning: reclining, lying down, supine, leaning back,
               flat on one's back
Derivation: Latin *recumbens,* prone
Examples:
      She remained in that recumbent position until she
      felt her back stiffen.
      No one supposed that the fighter enjoyed being
      recumbent so early in the fight.
recumbency *n.*

re-dun-dant *adj.*   *Pronunciation:* rē-dŭn'dŭnt
  Meaning: using more words than necessary, contain-
               ing something superfluous
Derivation: Latin *redundans,* overflowing
Examples:
      The editor said he didn't mind a few redundant
      phrases, but he hoped the author would keep them
      to a minimum.
      There were so many redundancies in her paper that
      the professor made her do it over.
redundancy and redundance *n.,* redundantly *adv.*

re-it-er-ate *v.t.*   *Pronunciation:* rē-ĭt'ēr-āt
  Meaning: to repeat, say or do over again repeatedly
Derivation: Latin *reiteratus*, spoken again
Examples:
      The lecturer reiterated each point so often that I
      almost fell asleep.

His point was, if you are going to reiterate anything, you had better reiterate the most important
points.

reiteration *n.*, reiterative *adj.*

re-ju-ve-nate *v.t.*   *Pronunciation:* rē-joo′vĕ-nāt
  Meaning: to render youthful again; to develop youth-
             ful features
  Derivation: Latin *rejuvenescere,* to become young again
  Examples:

  She thought that by going to the beauty parlor
  every week she would be rejuvenated.

  The Fountain of Youth was only the first in a long
  series of American rejuvenation hoaxes.

rejuvenation and rejuvenator *n.*

re-lent-less *adj.*   *Pronunciation:* rē-lĕnt′lĭs
  Meaning: merciless, uncompassionate
  Derivation: Latin *relentescere,* to grow soft + Anglo-
             Saxon *leas,* without
  Examples:

  She prodded the animal relentlessly because so
  much work was still undone.

  Inspector Maigret is described as a relentless pur-
  suer of criminals.

relentlessness *n.*, relentlessly *adv.*

re-pre-hen-si-ble *adj.*   *Pronunciation:*   rĕp-rē-hĕn′sĭ-bl
  Meaning: deserving censure, blameworthy
  Derivation: Late Latin *reprehensibilis,* blameworthy
  Examples:
      The higher court found the judge's behavior reprehensible and proposed a full investigation.
      He did not find the action as reprehensible as he thought he would.
reprehensibility *n.,* reprehensibly *adv.*

re-pu-di-ate *v.t.*   *Pronunciation:*   rĭ-pū′dĭ-āt
  Meaning: to refuse to acknowledge; to deny, disclaim; to refuse to accept as true or just
  Derivation: Latin *repudiātus,* rejected
  Examples:
      The senator's statement was repudiated by his office in time for the next edition of the newspaper.
      The representative has often repudiated his party's platform, but he has never resigned.
repudiation and repudiator *n.*

res-o-nance *n.*   *Pronunciation:*   rĕz′o-năns
  Meaning: resounding, sonorous, having the quality of prolonged sound
  Derivation: Latin *resonans,* resounding
  Examples:
      The new violin lacked the resonance of the great Italian instruments.
      The actor had a resonant voice that was heard in every part of the theater.
resonant *adj.,* resonantly *adv.*

re-sus-ci-tate *v.t., v.i.*　　*Pronunciation:*　rĕ-sŭs'ĭ-tāt

Meaning:　*v.t.* to bring back to life, restore after uncon-
sciousness or apparent death; *v.i.* to revive
after apparent death

Derivation:　Latin *resuscitātus,* revived

Examples:

v.t. The policemen took turns attempting to resusci-
tate the victim.

v.t. The liberal supply of stimulants resuscitated
the man.

v.i. The man resuscitated after most of the oxygen
had been exhausted.

resuscitation and resuscitator *n.,* resuscitative *adj.*

ret-i-cent *adj.*　　*Pronunciation:*　rĕt'ĭ-sĭnt

Meaning:　reserved, taciturn, sparing in communication

Derivation:　Latin *reticens,* being silent

Examples:

Under questioning by the police, the prisoner was
reticent about his past criminal activities.

Reticence is characteristic of the shy child.

reticence *n.,* reticently *adv.*

ret-ro-gress *v.i.*　　*Pronunciation:*　rĕt'rō-grĕs

Meaning:　to go back to an earlier condition; to move
backward

Derivation:　Latin *retrogradi,* to go back

Examples:
>   Do you consider that civilization has progressed or
>   retrogressed in the twentieth century?
>   One cannot retrogress even temporarily if sus-
>   tained improvement is a goal.

retrogression *n.,* retrograde *v.i.,* retrograde *adj.*

re-ver-ber-ate *v.i.*   *Pronunciation:*   rĕ-vŭr′ bĕr-āt
  Meaning: to be reflected; to rebound, resound
Derivation: Latin *reverberāre,* to strike back, repel
Examples:
>   After being struck, the bell reverberated for half a
>   minute.
>   These events are going to provide a constant deluge
>   of headlines and many political reverberations for
>   months to come.

reverberation *n.,* reverberative *adj.*

rib-ald *adj.*   *Pronunciation:*   rĭb′ld
  Meaning: coarse, licentious, obscene, low, scurrilous
Derivation: Old French *ribaut,* dissipate
Examples:
>   Ribald speech cannot be tolerated in a church.
>   His ribald wit offended many of us and made his
>   host uncomfortable.

ribaldry *n.*

ru-di-men-ta-ry *adj.* *Pronunciation:*   roō-dĭ-mĕn′tŭ-rē
  Meaning: elementary

Derivation: Latin *rudīmentum,* beginning
Examples:

This student's knowledge of grammar obviously has never gone beyond the rudimentary stage.

In my apprenticeship, I expect to learn more than the rudiments of the craft.

rudiment and rudimentariness *n.,* rudimentarily *adv.*

ru-mi-nate *v.t., v.i.*   *Pronunciation:* rōō′mĭ-nāt

Meaning: *v.t.* to think about again and again; *v.i.* to ponder

Derivation: Latin *ruminari,* to chew again that which has already been chewed, swallowed, and brought up again

Examples:

v.t. Her inclination to ruminate on the past was the despair of her friends, who urged her to forget old times and strike out boldly.

v.i. Men of action cannot afford to ruminate.

rumination *n.,* ruminative *adj.,* ruminatively *adv.*

sSs

sac-ro-sanct *adj.*   *Pronunciation:*   săk′rō-sănkt
  Meaning: most sacred (often used ironically)
Derivation: Latin *sacrōsanctus,* holiest
  Examples:

  Followers of the guru regard his every word as
  sacrosanct.

  Good reviewers do not treat new books as sacrosanct.

sacrosanctity *n.*

sa-la-cious *adj.* *Pronunciation:* să-lā′shŭs
  Meaning: lecherous, lustful
Derivation: Latin *salāx,* lustful; fond of leaping
Examples:

> The Supreme Court has refused to define what the law finds salacious, much to the disgust of the narrow-minded.
>
> An X rating designates films considered salacious.

salaciousness and salacity *n.,* salaciously *adv.*

sa-li-ent *adj.* *Pronunciation:* sā′lĭ-ĕnt
  Meaning: noticeable, prominent, conspicuous
Derivation: Latin *saliens,* leaping forth
Examples:

> The salient argument in the lawyer's summation stressed the defendant's poverty-stricken youth.
>
> Monet's depiction of nature is considered his salient artistic strength.

salience and saliency *n.,* saliently *adv.*

sanc-ti-mo-nious *adj.* *Pronunciation:* sănk-tĭ-mō′nĭ-ŭs
  Meaning: pretending piety or holiness
Derivation: Latin *sanctimōnia,* sacredness
Examples:

> I am tired of your sanctimonious ways, you old hypocrite.
>
> Her sanctimonious speech angered those of us who knew her true instincts.

sanctimony and sanctimoniousness *n.,* sanctimoniously *adv.*

san-guine *adj.*   *Pronunciation:*   săng′gwĭn
  Meaning: red; cheerful, optimistic; bloodthirsty
  Derivation: Latin *sanguineus,* bloody
  Examples:
      A sanguine complexion usually means good health.
      She was perfectly sanguine about her prospects,
      although I could not understand why.
      A samurai is generally portrayed as a sanguine
      warrior.
  sanguineness *n.,* sanguinary *adj.,* sanguinely *adv.*

sar-don-ic *adj.*   *Pronunciation:*   sär-dŏn′ĭk
  Meaning: scornful, disdainful
  Derivation: Greek *sardánios,* bitter
  Examples:
      The comedian's sardonic wit caused the audience
      considerable discomfort.
      A sardonic manner does not win friends.
  sardonically *adv.*

scur-ril-ous *adj.*   *Pronunciation:*   skŭr′ĭ-lŭs
  Meaning: inclined to obscene jokes or offensive re-
              marks; offensive, coarse
  Derivation: Latin *scurra,* buffoon, jester
  Examples:
      The attorney called the press conference to label
      these rumors false and scurrilous.
      Scurrilousness is not condoned in my home or any-
      where else I go.
  scurrility and scurrilousness *n.,* scurrilously *adv.*

sed-en-tar-y *adj.*   *Pronunciation:* sĕd'ĕn-tĕr-ē
 Meaning: stationary, sitting, inactive
Derivation: Latin *sedentārius* from *sedere,* to sit
Examples:

> Sedentary jobs are not sought after by vigorous men and women.

> In bad weather, the sedentary life John led had its rewards.

sedentariness *n.,* sedentarily *adv.*

se-nile *adj.*   *Pronunciation:* sē'nīl, sē'nĭl
 Meaning: characteristic of old age and its infirmities
Derivation: Latin *senex,* old man
Examples:

> Senile people have no place in some cultures.

> His developing senility was obvious to all his friends.

senility *n.*

sen-ten-tious *adj.*   *Pronunciation:* sĕn-tĕn'shŭs
 Meaning: given to pithy sayings; given to an excessive use of wise sayings
Derivation: Latin *sententiōsus,* pithy, full of meaning
Examples:

> I cannot sit much longer through Professor Allen's sententious lectures.

> Why must he drone on and on sententiously to the obvious discomfort of his audience?

sententiousness *n.,* sententiously *adv.*

snide *adj.*   *Pronunciation:* snīd'
  Meaning: subtly sarcastic
  Derivation: Anglo-Saxon *snīthan,* to cut
  Examples:

    Sooner or later, your snide remarks will bring about your dismissal.

    The reviewer hinted snidely that the author misused his sources.

snidely *adv.*

som-no-lent *adj.*   *Pronunciation:* sŏm'nō-lĕnt
  Meaning: sleepy, drowsy
  Derivation: Latin *somnolentus,* sleepy
  Examples:

    The side streets of Scarsdale are almost deserted on somnolent afternoons in August.

    Somnolent students sit patiently through their classes, totally unaware of what the lecturer is saying.

soph-o-mor-ic *adj.*   *Pronunciation:* sŏf-ō-mô'rĭk
  Meaning: immature, shallow
  Derivation: Greek *sophos,* wise + *mōros,* foolish
  Examples:

    I found him insufferably sophomoric.

    Sophomoric statements are characteristic of minds unencumbered by useful knowledge.

sophomorically *adv.*

so·po·rif·ic *n., adj.*   *Pronunciation:* sŏ-pô-rĭf'ĭk
  Meaning: *n.* a substance that induces sleep; *adj.* caus-
              ing sleep, sleepy
  Derivation: Latin *soporifer,* that which induces sleep
  Examples:

    n. The novels of Bulwer-Lytton are my favorite
    soporific, capable of inducing snores within five
    minutes.

    adj. Such long-winded, soporific suggestions are
    useless if we are to sway the committee.

sor·did *adj.*   *Pronunciation:* sôr'dĭd
  Meaning: filthy, dirty, vile, base, gross
  Derivation: Latin *sordere,* to be dirty
  Examples:

    His arrest came after a series of sordid episodes that
    captured the attention of the tabloid newspapers.

    Zola's novels portray the sordidness of Paris in the
    nineteenth century.

  sordidness *n.,* sordidly *adv.*

spe·cious *adj.*   *Pronunciation:* spē'shŭs
  Meaning: outwardly pleasing, showy; apparently but
              deceptively just, fair, or correct
  Derivation: Latin *speciōsus,* good-looking

Examples:

Such specious comparisons were not worthy of the speaker, who should have had higher regard for his audience.

That kind of specious reasoning will never get you into graduate school.

speciousness and speciosity *n.*, speciously *adv.*

spu-ri-ous *adj.*   *Pronunciation:* spū'rĭ-ŭs
  Meaning: not genuine, counterfeit, false
Derivation: Latin *spurius,* false
  Examples:

They wondered how long the supervisor could detain the client on such a spurious excuse.

The lawyer for the defense called the charges spurious and misleading.

spuriousness *n.*, spuriously *adv.*

stip-u-late *v.t.*   *Pronunciation:* stĭp'ū-lāt
  Meaning: to bargain; to contract; to insist upon, demand, require
Derivation: Latin *stipulātus,* past part. of *stipulari,* to establish agreement
  Examples:

When he ordered dinner, he stipulated imported beer rather than the inferior domestic brew.

It was stipulated in the contract that the payments were to be made quarterly.

stipulation and stipulator *n.*

stri-dent *adj.*   *Pronunciation:*   strī'dĕnt

  Meaning: harsh-sounding, grating, shrill

  Derivation: Latin *strīdens,* creaking

  Examples:

    The old man's strident voice caused echoes in the laboratory.

    The two crickets made strident sounds incessantly and kept us up for hours.

  stridence and stridency *n.,* stridently *adv.*

strin-gent *adj.*   *Pronunciation:*   strĭn'jĕnt

  Meaning: strict, rigid, thoroughgoing, exacting

  Derivation: Latin *stringens,* drawing tight

  Examples:

    The Dean imposed a curfew at 7:00, the most stringent curb on the student's liberty that she felt she could supervise.

    This was the most stringent regulation the broker had ever encountered.

  stringency *n.,* stringently *adv.*

stul-ti-fy *v.t.*   *Pronunciation:*   stŭl'tĭ-fī

  Meaning: to make or cause to appear stupid, make a fool of; to frustrate, invalidate, or reduce to futility

  Derivation: Latin *stultus,* foolish + *fy,* cause

Examples:

The veto provision stultifies the reconstruction program that the U.N. had undertaken in Africa.

The faculty became impatient with some of the stultifying tactics of the Board of Trustees.

stultification and stultifier *n.*

sub-ser-vi-ent *adj.*   *Pronunciation:*   sŭb-sŭrv′yĕnt
  Meaning: useful in an inferior capacity, menial, slavish
Derivation: Latin *subserviens,* serving under
  Examples:

Governors tend to be subservient to legislators when seeking some pet project.

The class believed that no one should be subservient to anyone else.

subservience and subserviency *n.*, subserviently *adv.*

sub-stan-ti-ate *v.t.*   *Pronunciation:*   sŭb-stăn′shĭ-āt
  Meaning: to verify, confirm, bear out by evidence, prove to be true, authenticate, validate
Derivation: Latin *sub,* under + *stare,* to stand
  Examples:

That statement was substantiated by the evidence presented to the jury.

The archaeologist substantiated his claim of being first on the site by producing a jaw bone in excellent condition.

substantiation *n.*, substantiative *adj.*

sub-ter-fuge *n.*   *Pronunciation:* sŭb′tēr-fūj

Meaning: deception, plan for escaping censure or evading an issue

Derivation: Latin *subterfugere,* to flee secretly, escape

Examples:

> She used every subterfuge she knew of, but he was relentless in his pursuit of her.

> The lawyer was uncertain whether his subterfuge would work, but he certainly was going to try it.

sub-tle-ty *n.*   *Pronunciation:* sŭt′l-tĭ

Meaning: fine point, nicety, delicacy, finely drawn distinction

Derivation: Latin *subtilis,* thin, fine, delicate

Examples:

> The reasoning behind the statement showed a mind of great subtetly.

> The subtle accusation at first aroused no antagonism in him because he did not grasp its full meaning.

subtleness *n.,* subtle *adj.,* subtly *adv.*

t T t

tac-i-turn *adj.*   *Pronunciation:* tăs′ĭ-tûrn

   Meaning: habitually silent, not given to conversing
Derivation: Latin *taciturnus,* silent
   Examples:

   John Wayne often portrays taciturn characters in
   his pictures.
   Helen was one of those rare people who are taciturn
   by nature and inclination.

taciturnity *n.,* taciturnly *adv.*

tan-gi-ble *adj.*   *Pronunciation:* tăn′jĭ-bl
  Meaning: capable of being touched, perceptible to the
               touch; real or actual rather than imaginary
  Derivation: Latin *tangibilis* from *tangere,* to touch
  Examples:

    The application for the loan was turned down be-
    cause the applicant had no tangible assets.

    The interviewer explained all the tangible benefits
    that the applicant would receive if she joined the
    firm.

tangibility and tangibleness *n.,* tangibly *adv.*

tan-ta-lize *v.t.*   *Pronunciation:* tăn′tŭ-līz
  Meaning: to vex, tease, provoke, torment; to punish by
               showing a desired object but keeping it out of
               reach
  Derivation: Greek *Tantalus,* son of Zeus and the nymph
                  Pluto, who was condemned to stand in water
                  up to his chin and unable to reach a fruit tree
                  above him
  Examples:

    The Vice President explained that he had called the
    conference in order to solve some tantalizing prob-
    lems that threatened economic stability.

    The poor girl stood in front of the shop window,
    tantalized by the expensive dresses displayed be-
    fore her eyes.

tantalizer and tantalization *n.*, tantalizing *adj.*, tantaliz-
ingly *adv.*

tan-ta-mount *adj.*   *Pronunciation:* tăn'tŭ-mount
  Meaning: equivalent in value, meaning, or effect
Derivation: Latin *tantum,* so much + English amount
  Examples:
       What she said concerning her hatred of the dead
       man was tantamount to a confession.
       Abandoning the property was tantamount to relin-
       quishing all rights of ownership.

te-di-ous *adj.*   *Pronunciation:* tē'dĭ-ŭs, tē'jŭs
  Meaning: tiresome, wearisome, irksome, boring,
              monotonous, humdrum
Derivation: Latin *taediōsus,* tiresome
  Examples:
       She believed that the term paper was the most
       tedious assignment she had ever had in college and
       was without any educational value.
       The conference was so tedious and the room so
       warm that half the participants nearly fell asleep.
tediousness *n.,* tediously *adv.*

te-na-cious *adj.*   *Pronunciation:* tĕ-nā'shŭs
  Meaning: holding fast or inclined to hold fast; highly
              retentive
Derivation: Latin *tenāx* from *tenere,* to hold
  Examples:
       The mountain climber had a tenacious grip on the
       rope.
       He had a tenacious mind that was the envy of his
       colleagues.
tenaciousness and tenacity *n.,* tenaciously *adv.*

ten-ta-tive *adj.*   *Pronunciation:*   těn′tŭ-tĭv

  Meaning: experimental, offered or undertaken provi-
               sionally

Derivation: Latin *tentātīvus* from *tentāre,* to try

  Examples:

    The lecturer explained that the plan for the festival
    was only tentative.

    We made tentative plans to meet in London later in
    the year, not knowing whether they ever would be
    realized.

tentativeness *n.,* tentatively *adv.*

tim-or-ous *adj.*   *Pronunciation:*   tǐm′ĕr-ŭs

  Meaning: fearful, timid, cowering, apprehensive, eas-
               ily alarmed

Derivation: Latin *timorōsus,* frightened

  Examples:

    The person you introduced me to is the most timor-
    ous individual I have ever met.

    Many rodents are timorous by nature, fleeing at the
    slightest sign of danger.

timorousness *n.,* timorously *adv.*

tor-ment *v.t.*   *Pronunciation:*   tôr-měnt′

  Meaning: to cause acute physical or mental anguish; to
               vex, harass; to agitate

Derivation: Old French *tormenter,* to afflict with pain

Examples:

The detective tormented the criminal by not permitting him to smoke during the interrogation.

In some English schools, the older boys torment the younger ones.

torment *n.,* tormentingly *adv.*

tra-verse *v.t.*   *Pronunciation:* tră′ vĕrs, tră-vĕrs′

Meaning: to pass through or across; to move backwards and forwards

Derivation: French *traverser,* to cross

Examples:

The patrolmen traversed the area again and again without finding the murder weapon.

The travelers traversed some of the most treacherous terrain they had ever encountered but finally reached their destination safely.

traverser *n.,* traversable *adj.*

trep-i-da-tion *n.*   *Pronunciation:* trĕp-ĭ-dā′shŭn

Meaning: a quaking or involuntary trembling; a state of alarm or fear

Derivation: Latin *trepidātio,* hurrying; being alarmed

Examples:

Frances was filled with trepidation before the interview, fearing that she would not get the job.

The trepidation he felt was unjustified, since no one was charging him with anything.

trun-cate *v.t.*   *Pronunciation:*   trŭng′kāt
   Meaning: to lessen by cutting; to lop off
   Derivation: Latin *truncātus,* past part. of *truncāre,* to cut
                   off, mutilate
   Examples:
         The violence of the wind truncated every tree in the
         area.
         The horns truncated the development of the major
         theme by the violins.
   truncation *n.,* truncated *adj.*

tu-mul-tu-ous *adj.*   *Pronunciation:*   tū-mŭl′choo-ŭs
   Meaning: full of turbulence, commotion, or agitation
   Derivation: Latin *tumultuōsus,* noisy
   Examples:
         The King received a tumultuous welcome from the
         citizens of London on his return from France.
         Willie Mays received a tumultuous ovation on his
         last day as a baseball player.
   tumultuousness *n.,* tumultuously *adv.*

u **U** u

u-biq-ui-tous *adj.*   *Pronunciation:*   ū-bĭk′wĭ-tŭs
  Meaning: present everywhere (usually intended in a
               humorous sense)
  Derivation: Latin *ubique*, everywhere
  Examples:
          The ubiquitous pizza parlor appears to be feeding
          America.
          Wherever we walked in the meadow, we found the
          ubiquitous ragweed.
  ubiquity and ubiquitousness *n.*, ubiquitously *adv.*

unc-tu-ous *adj.*   *Pronunciation:* ŭnk′chōo-ŭs
  Meaning: oily; overly suave, hypocritically warm
  Derivation: Latin *unctuōsus,* annointed
  Examples:

> The unctuous manner in which the host greeted his guests offended many of them.
> What some people perceive as sophistication is seen by others as unctuousness.

unctuousness and unctuosity *n.,* unctuously *adv.*

un-du-late *v.i.*   *Pronunciation:* ŭn′dū-lāt
  Meaning: move like a wave
  Derivation: Latin *unda,* wave
  Examples:

> Many diners ignored their meals when the Oriental dancer began to undulate in time with the music.
> The undulation of the hills north of London gives the impression of an ocean of green grass.

undulation *n.,* undulated *adj.*

u-ni-lat-er-al *adj.*   *Pronunciation:* ū-nĭ-lăt′ĕr-ŭl
  Meaning: one-sided; affecting only one side of a question or dispute
  Derivation: Latin *uni,* one + *latus,* side
  Examples:

> Unilateral agreements are really never binding.
> Mediators in labor disputes try to prevent unilateral actions that would impede negotiations leading to satisfaction of the claims of both management and labor.

unilaterally *adv.*

un-ob-tru-sive *adj.*   *Pronunciation:* ŭn-ŏb-tro͞o′sĭv
  Meaning: not inclined to prominence, retiring
  Derivation: Latin *in,* not + *obtrudere,* thrust
  Examples:
      Sally's unobtrusive manner pleased her friends but
      did little for her business career.
      Certain religions encourage unobtrusiveness as a
      sign of humility and godliness.
  unobtrusiveness *n.,* unobtrusively *adv.*

un-sa-vor-y *adj.*   *Pronunciation:* ŭn-sā′vō-rē
  Meaning: having a disagreeable taste or odor; suggest-
          ing something disagreeable or even morally
          bad
  Derivation: Middle English *un,* not + *savure,* fragrant
  Examples:
      The young chefs risk an unsavory meal when they
      decide they know more than the master chef.
      A careful defense attorney will insist on keeping his
      client off the witness stand to prevent exposure of
      any unsavory reputation.
  unsavoriness *n.,* unsavorily *adv.*

un-ten-able *adj.*   *Pronunciation:*   ŭn-tĕn′ŭ-bl
  Meaning: incapable of being defended or maintained
  Derivation: Latin *un,* not + *tenere,* hold
  Examples:
      Major Dyer advised his commanding officer that
      the battalion's position was untenable and
      suggested an immediate withdrawal.

I wish you would not waste our time with long-winded arguments supporting untenable propositions.

untenability and untenableness *n.*

un-wield-y *adj.*   *Pronunciation:* ŭn-wēld-ē
   Meaning: clumsy, bulky, manageable only with difficulty
   Derivation: Anglo-Saxon *wealdon,* govern
   Examples:
      Moving men are accustomed to handling objects you and I would consider unwieldy.
      Corporations often employ unwieldy procedures that sensible men and women would avoid.
   unwieldiness *n.,* unwieldily *adv.*

up-braid *v.t.*   *Pronunciation:* ŭp-brād′
   Meaning: to accuse or criticize someone severely
   Derivation: Anglo-Saxon *upbregdan,* to draw or twist
   Examples:
      The teacher upbraided the entire class for lack of interest in school work.
      We must be careful not to upbraid children for every mistake they make.
   upbraider *n.*

ur-bane *adj.*   *Pronunciation:* ŭr-bān′
   Meaning: refined in manners, courteous, suave, polished
   Derivation: Latin *urbānus,* of a city

Examples:

All though his adolescence, John had no higher ambition than to be thought of as urbane.

Oscar Wilde's urbanity impressed even his detractors.

urbanity and urbaneness *n.*, urbanely *adv.*

u-surp *v.t.*   *Pronunciation:* ū-zŭrp′
  Meaning: to seize and hold without legal authority, take possession of by force
Derivation: Latin *ūsurpāre,* to seize
  Examples:

Citizens must be alert to any attempt to usurp the authority of the courts.

The President of the United States was accused in the press of an unprecedented usurpation and misuse of power.

usurpation and usurper *n.*

u-til-i-ta-ri-an *adj.*   *Pronunciation:* ū-tĭl-ĭ-tă′rē-ŭn
  Meaning: based on usefulness as the prime consideration
Derivation: Latin *ūtilitas,* usefulness
  Examples:

Karl Marx advocated a utilitarian approach to management of a nation's economy.

The nineteenth century saw great interest in utilitarianism among many prominent intellectuals, led by John Stuart Mill.

utilitarianism *n.*

vac-u-ous *adj.*   *Pronunciation:*   văk′ū-ŭs

  Meaning: empty, vacant, blank; stupid, dull, unintelligent

Derivation: Latin *vacuus,* empty

Examples:

Half the workers in the factory walk around with vacuous expressions on their faces, bored by the dulling repetitiveness of their jobs.

The paintings in the exhibition seemed to her to be devoid of interest, vacuous, and uninventive.

vacuousness *n.,* vacuously *adv.*

va-pid *adj.*   *Pronunciation:*   vă′pĭd
  Meaning: having lost its life, spirit or zest; dull, spirit-
    less, inane
  Derivation: Latin *vapidus,* that which has exhaled its
    vapor
  Examples:
    The guest speaker made one of the most vapid
    speeches the audience had ever heard.
    Even though everyone was thirsty, no one would
    drink the vapid beer.
vapidity and vapidness *n.,* vapidly *adv.*

ve-he-ment *adj.*   *Pronunciation:*   vē′hĕ-mĕnt
  Meaning: acting with great force; furious, impetuous,
    urgent
  Derivation: French *véhément,* vehement
  Examples:
    The truckers staged a vehement protest meeting,
    which ended in a march through the streets.
    The vehemence of his reply astounded all who know
    him as a meek person.
vehemence *n.,* vehemently *adv.*

ver-bose *adj.*   *Pronunciation:*   vĕr-bōs′
  Meaning: wordy, prolix, redundant, uninteresting be-
    cause of the overuse of words
  Derivation: Latin *verbum,* word
  Examples:
    College professors are among the most verbose
    people on earth.

The lecturer's verbosity put the audience to sleep.
verboseness and verbosity *n.*, verbosely *adv.*

ves-tige *n.*   *Pronunciation:* věs′tĭj

Meaning: trace, mark, or visible sign of something perished or lost, remaining bit

Derivation: Latin *vestīgium,* footprint, sign

Examples:

After it had rained on and off for a week, not a vestige of the snow remained, and the grass began to grow.

The glaciers that covered the Eastern seaboard left vestigial traces on the rocks in the Ramapo mountains.

vestigial *adj.*, vestigially *adv.*

vi-a-ble *adj.*   *Pronunciation:* vī′ŭ-bl

Meaning: capable of growing and developing; capable of living

Derivation: French *vie,* life, from Latin *vita*

Examples:

The first question he asked the grower was whether the seeds were viable.

She wondered whether a rational and politically viable group would ever attempt to overthrow the student government.

viability *n.*

vi-car-i-ous *adj.*   *Pronunciation:* vī-kă′rĭ-ŭs

Meaning: delegated, deputed, substituted, acting for another

Derivation: Latin *vicārius,* substituted
  Examples:

> Do we receive vicarious pleasure from watching a
> movie love scene?
> A vicarious sacrifice was substituted for animal
> sacrifice as the religion developed.

vicariousness *n.,* vicariously *adv.*

vil-i-fy *v.t.*   *Pronunciation:*   vĭl'ĭ-fī
  Meaning: to degrade or debase by report, defame,
                speak evil of
Derivation: Late Latin *vīlificāre,* defame
  Examples:

> The newspaper vilified the officer for the way he
> handled the situation.
> He was so hurt by her behavior that he believed
> everything that was said to vilify her.

vilification and vilifier *n.*

vin-dic-tive *adj.*   *Pronunciation:*   vĭn-dĭk'tĭv
  Meaning: revengeful, prompted or characterized by
                revenge
Derivation: Latin *vindicta,* revenge
  Examples:

> The vindictive nature of their remarks indicated
> that the leaders of the opposition would have plenty
> of ammunition for the next political campaign.
> The man's remarks were so vindictive that the
> clerk could scarcely contain his fears.

vindictiveness *n.,* vindictively *adv.*

vi-ti-ate *v.t.*   *Pronunciation:* vĭsh'ĭ-āt
  Meaning: to contaminate, spoil, corrupt, pollute
Derivation: Latin *vitiātus,* spoiled
  Examples:

> The lawyer pointed out that the fraud vitiated the contract, and nothing could be done about it.

> She went to see so many bad plays that they vitiated her critical sense.

vitiation and vitiator *n.*

vi-tu-per-ate *v.t.*   *Pronunciation:* vī-tū' pĕr-āt
  Meaning: to abuse with words, censure severely, berate
Derivation: Latin *vituperatus,* blamed
  Examples:

> The barrister vituperated the handling of the case by the prosecuting attorney.

> The man used such vituperative language in court that the judge ordered him removed.

vituperative *adj.,* vituperatively *adv.*

vi-va-cious *adj.*   *Pronunciation:* vĭ-vā'shŭs
  Meaning: lively in temper or conduct, sprightly
Derivation: Latin *vivax* from *vivere,* to live
  Examples:

> She had the kind of vivacious personality that attracts people.

> The lecturer spoke in a manner so vivacious that many students were attracted to her classes.

vivacity and vivaciousness *n.,* vivaciously *adv.*

vo-cif-er-ous *adj.*   *Pronunciation:* vō-sĭf'ēr-ŭs
  Meaning: making a loud outcry, noisy, boisterous
  Derivation: Latin *vōciferātus,* past part. of *vōciferāri,* to
               shout
  Examples:
        Many of the fans in the stands became vociferous as
        the game became more lively.
        They responded vociferously when the cheerleaders
        appealed to them.
  vociferousness *n.,* vociferously *adv.*

vo-li-tion *n.*   *Pronunciation:*   vō-lĭsh'ŭn
  Meaning: the act of willing or choosing; exercise of the
               will, determination of an act of willing or
               choosing
  Derivation: Middle Latin *volitio* from *volo,* I wish
  Examples:
        They made the choice to go of their own volition.
        She decided of her own volition to take a year off
        from college and see what it felt like to work for a
        while.
  volitional and volitionary *adj.,* volitionally *adv.*

vol-u-ble *adj.*   *Pronunciation:* vŏl'ū-bl
  Meaning: fluent and smooth in speech, glib, garrulous
  Derivation: Latin *volūbilis* from *volvere,* to roll, turn
               around
  Examples:
        They both counted on his voluble nature to get them
        out of the jam.

The intern spoke with such volubleness that even
the patients who knew him well were amazed.

volubleness and volubility *n.,* volubly *adv.*

vo-ra-cious *adj.*   *Pronunciation:*   vō-rā'shŭs

  Meaning: very hungry, ravenous

Derivation: Latin *vorācitas,* greediness

  Examples:

The tackle on the football team had such a voracious appetite that he was always eating.

The teacher was a voracious reader of mystery
novels, but he hated to read student themes.

voraciousness and voracity *n.,* voraciously *adv.*

wan-ton *adj.*   *Pronunciation:* wŏn′tŭn

  Meaning: unchaste, lewd, licentious, malicious; having no real provocation

  Derivation: Middle English *wantoun,* undisciplined

  Examples:

    The jailer was accused of wanton cruelty.

    Jane felt that she could not ignore such a wanton insult.

wantonness *n.,* wantonly *adv.*

war-y *adj.*   *Pronunciation:*   wăr'ē
  Meaning: cautious of danger, careful, guarded
  Derivation: Anglo-Saxon *waer,* watchful
  Examples:
    Many small animals are wary of the larger pre-
    dators.
    All these incidents made them wary of any pre-
    cipitous action.
wariness *n.,* warily *adv.*

wa-ver *v.i.*   *Pronunciation:*   wā'vĕr
  Meaning: to vacillate, be unsettled in opinion; to falter
  Derivation: Old Norse *vafra,* move unsteadily
  Examples:
    The front line wavered under the fire of the artil-
    lery.
    She wavered between two alternatives—either to
    accept his proposal or to reject it.
waverer *n.,* wavering *adj.,* waveringly *adv.*

way-lay *v.t.*   *Pronunciation:*   wā-lā'
  Meaning: to lie in wait for; to take steps to encounter
        someone or something, especially with a
        view to robbing or seizing
  Derivation: German *wegelagern,* to await
  Examples:
    The drunken sailors were waylaid on the way back
    to the ship.
    The robbers hoped to waylay the shipment in the
    hills and escape by helicopter.
waylayer *n.*

way-ward *adj.*   *Pronunciation:* wā'wẽrd
  Meaning: taking one's own way, disobedient; fluctuat-
              ing, irregular
  Derivation: Middle English *weiward,* in a direction
              away from a thing
  Examples:
      He was struck by a wayward pitch and suffered a
      broken arm.
      A wayward son brings no joy to his family.
  waywardness *n.,* waywardly *adv.*

whim-sy *n.*   *Pronunciation:* hwĭm'zĭ
  Meaning: caprice, vagary; fanciful or fantastic speech
              or actions
  Derivation: Norwegian *kvimsa,* flutter about
  Examples:
      The most noted characteristic of his novels was
      their whimsy.
      The whimsical nature of the play appealed to most
      of the audience, who were tired of the heavy tragedy
      of most of the season's plays.
  whimisicality and whimsicalness *n.,* whimsical *adj.,*
  whimsically *adv.*

wil-y *adj.*   *Pronunciation:* wīl'ē
  Meaning: crafty, sly
  Derivation: Anglo-Saxon *wīle,* trick
  Examples:
      The manager was wily in interviewing applicants
      for the job; he wanted to employ someone who was
      well qualified but would work for low pay.

Only the wily fox catches the fleet rabbits.
wiliness *n.*, wilily *adv.*

win-some *adj.* *Pronunciation:* wĭn´sŭm
  Meaning: cheerful, merry, gay, causing joy or pleasure
Derivation: Anglo-Saxon *wynsum,* joyous
  Examples:
    A winsome smile was her greatest asset.
    She sang so winsomely that the audience glowed
    with pleasure.
winsomeness *n.*, winsomely *adv.*

woe-ful *adj.* *Pronunciation:* wō´fŭl
  Meaning: paltry, miserable, sorrowful
Derivation: Anglo-Saxon *wā,* sorrow
  Examples:
    The audience thought that the song recital was the
    most woeful offering of the season.
    She had such a woeful expression on her face that I
    felt sorry for her in spite of myself.
woefulness *n.*, woefully *adv.*

wrath *n.* *Pronunciation:* răth´
  Meaning: violent anger, rage
Derivation: Anglo-Saxon *wraethu,* anger

Examples:
> The teacher's wrath turned the whole class into obedient but frightened students.
>
> When he found he could not recover the stolen money, he went into a wrathful state.

wrathfulness *n.*, wrathful *adj.*, wrathfully *adv.*

xen-o-pho-bi-a *n.*   *Pronunciation:*   zĕn-o-fō'bĭ-ă

  Meaning: fear or hatred of foreigners

Derivation: Greek *xénos,* stranger + *phobia,* fear

  Examples:

    People have always accused the French of
xenophobia.

    Many politicians have built their careers by
exploiting the xenophobia of their constituents.

xenophobic *adj.*

y Y y

yearn *v.i.*   *Pronunciation:* yûrn′
  Meaning: to be filled with longing
Derivation: Middle English *yerne,* desire
Examples:
    The child yearned for toys she could not have.
    All his yearning only resulted in fits of despondency
    that grew more and more frequent with time.
yearning *n.*, yearningly *adv.*

z Z z

zeal *n.*   *Pronunciation:* zēl′

 Meaning: ardent pursuit of something, eagerness, enthusiasm

Derivation: Greek *zēlos,* ardor

Examples:

 They attacked the problem with such zeal that the solution was simple.

 If he showed as much zeal for work as he did for play, he would be a rich man.

zeal-ot *n.*   *Pronunciation:*   zĕl'ŭt
  Meaning: a fanatical partisan
Derivation: Late Latin *zēlotēs,* zealots
  Examples:

    He was the greatest zealot in the movement and the
    logical choice for an act of fanaticism.

    To be as ardent as she over so small a matter, you
    have to be a zealot.

zeal-ous *adj.*   *Pronunciation:*   zĕl'ŭs
  Meaning: filled with or characterized by zeal
Derivation: Middle Latin *zēlōsus,* zealous
  Examples:

    The class was the most zealous she had ever en-
    countered.

    He is always zealous in pursuit of his goals, which is
    why he is so successful.

zealousness *n.,* zealously *adv.*

Appendix
Common Prefixes and Suffixes

Prefix	Meaning	Sample Words
a, an	without, not	abyss, amoral, anarchy, anhydrous
ab, abs	off, away from	aberrant, absence, abstain
ad, ac, ag, al, an, as, at	to (The basic form *ad* changes to *ac, ag, al, an, as,* or *at* before root words beginning with certain consonants.)	admit, adapt, accept, aggravate, allow, annotate, assure, attract
ambi, amphi	both, around, on both sides	ambidextrous, ambient, amphitheater, amphibious
ana	up, throughout, upon, again	anagram, analogy, anathema, anachronism
ante	before in space or time	antebellum, antedate, antecedent, antediluvian
anti	against, opposite, opposed to	anticlerical, anticipate, antibody, antihistamine
apo	from, away, off	apology, apostrophe
bi	twice, two	biweekly, bisect, biennial, bicycle
cata	down, against, back	catastrophe, cataract
circum	around	circumnavigate, circumvent
com, con co, cog, col, cor	together or with (The basic form *com* changes to *con, co, cog, col,* or *cor* before root words	commute, commit, confer, convene, cohabit, cooperate, cognate, collect,

181

Prefix	Meaning	Sample Words
	beginning with certain consonants.)	collate, correspond, correlate
contra, contro, counter	against, opposing, opposite	contradiction, controversy, counterespionage
de	from, off, down	detract, descend, debar, decision
demi	half	demitasse
di	twice, two	divide, dihedral
dia	across, through, thorough	diagonal, dialogue, diameter, diathermy
dis, dif, di	apart, away, not (The basic form *dis* changes to *dif* before words beginning with *f*. It also changes to *di* before certain other consonants.)	disappear, dissemble, dissect, differ, difficult, direct, digest
ex, e	from, out of, thoroughly (The basic form *ex* changes to *e* before certain consonants.)	except, expel, emit, emote
epi	on, among, over, beside, to, against	epilogue, epigram, epidermis, epigraph
extra, extro	outside, beyond	extrapolate, extravagant, extrovert
hemi, semi, demi	half	hemisphere, semimonthly demigod
hyper	over, too much	hyperacidity, hyperbole
in, im, il, ir	not (The basic form *in* changes to *im*, *il*, or *ir* before certain consonants.)	incontrovertible, impossible, illiterate, irreducible
in, im	in (The basic form *in* changes to *im* before certain consonants.)	ingest, imbibe
inter, intro	between, among, together	interstellar, intersperse, introvert, introduce
juxta	near, close to	juxtapose

Prefix	Meaning	Sample Words
mal	bad, wrong	malcontent, malicious
mis	ill, wrong	mistake, misnomer, mischance
mono	one	mononucleosis, monomer, monocle, monosyllable
multi	many	multiply, multilateral
non	not	nonfunctional, nonconformist, noncombatant
ob, oc, of, op	toward, against, to, on over (The basic form *ob* changes to *oc, of,* or *op* before certain consonants.)	objective, obdurate, occlude, occasion, offer, offend, opportunity, oppose
para	near, beyond, beside	paramilitary, paradox, paragraph
per	throughout, through, completely, very	persuade, perennial, perceive, percussion
poly	many	polyandry, polygamy, polygraph
post	after, behind	postscript, postpone
pre	before, earlier	preclude, prevent, precede
pro	for	pro-labor, pro-American
pro	before in space or time	proceed, prologue
re	again, back	reseed, recede, recidivist, reinvent
retro	backward	retrogress, retroactive
sub, suc, suf, sug, sup, sur	under (The basic form *sub* changes to *suc, suf, sug, sup,* or *sur* before certain consonants.)	submarine, subsistence, succulent, succinct, suffer, suffocate, suggest, support, suppose, surrogate, surrender
super, sur	over in space, size, or quality	supernumerary, superman, supervisor, supersede, surround, surprise, survey

Prefix	Meaning	Sample Words
syn, sym, syl, sys	together or with (The basic form *syn* changes to *sym*, *syl*, or *sys* before certain consonants.)	synchronize, synergistic, symbol, symphony, syllable, syllogism, system
trans	across, beyond	transoceanic, transport, transcept, transfer
ultra	beyond, excessive	ultramontane, ultraconservative
un	not, reversal	unnecessary, unadorned, undo, unfasten

Suffix	Meaning	Sample Words
able	capable of	capable, attainable
ac	pertaining to	insomniac, cardiac
acy	state or quality of	democracy, lunacy
age	state or act of	portage, dotage
al	relating to	anal, rebuttal
an	relating to	plebeian, historian
ana	pertaining to a collection	Americana, Mozartiana
ance	state or quality of	distance, sustenance
ancy	state or quality of	dormancy, hesitancy
ant	quality of	dormant, defiant
ant	one who	postulant, defendant
ar	pertaining to, like	insular, rectangular
ar	one who	beggar, scholar
arium	a place for something	terrarium, planetarium
ary	related to	elementary, honorary
ary	a place for something	mortuary, commissary
ate	to cause	educate, ameliorate
ate	quality of	temperate, disconsolate
ate	office	doctorate, delegate
ation	cause or act of causing	decoration, elevation
ative	tendency, inclination	negative, decorative
cle	diminutive (something that indicates small size)	follicle, article
cule, culus	diminutive	molecule, homunculus
cy	state or quality of	dormancy, solvency
cy	office	presidency, captaincy
ee	one who receives an action	legatee, donee
eer	one who	mutineer, privateer
el	diminutive	carrel, model
en	constructed of	earthen, wooden
en	to make	shorten, widen
ence	state or quality of	affluence, diffidence
ency	state or quality of	fluency, currency
ent	quality of	negligent, indolent
er	one who, that which	maker, carpenter, answer, rubber
er	more (comparative degree)	better, sleepier
esce	to begin to be	convalesce, phosphoresce
escent	beginning to be, one who begins to be	pubescent, adolescent, convalescent, senescent
escence	state of beginning to be	adolescence, senescence

Suffix	Meaning	Sample Words
esque	resembling, in a particular style	picturesque, burlesque, romanesque, Dantesque
ess	female performer of action	actress, goddess
est	most (superlative degree)	finest, quickest
et, ette	diminutive	cigaret, cigarette
eur	one who	poseur, amateur
fy	to make or do	magnify, putrefy
ial	concerning	sacrificial, judicial
ian	belonging to	Armenian, Slovenian
ible	capable of	frangible, discernible
ic	belonging to, pertaining to	Hispanic, Homeric
ic	concerning, characterized by	altruistic, cosmic, dogmatic, comic
ical	related to, characterized by	economical, physical, inimical, grammatical
ice	state or quality of	avarice, poultice
ier	one who	grenadier, bombardier
ile	characterized by, resembling	tactile, febrile, servile, puerile
ine	resembling, characterized by	leonine, feline, adamantine, pristine
ion	state of, act of	confusion, conflagration, creation, indignation
ish	resembling	doltish, boorish
ism	state of being, doctrine	colloquialism, heroism, communism, fascism
ist	one who	hedonist, altruist
ite	native of	Hittite, Israelite
itis	inflammation	hepatitis, conjunctivitis
ive	characterized by	superlative, native
ize	to do or make	hypnotize, energize
ly	resembling	comely, motherly
ment	state, result of making	abandonment, merriment, decrement, fragment
mony	result	acrimony, hegemony
ness	state or quality of	happiness, tenderness
oid	resembling	anthropoid, hominoid

Suffix	Meaning	Sample Words
or	one who	doctor, censor
or	state of	humor, languor
orium	a place for something	auditorium, crematorium
ory	a place for something	lavatory, dormitory
ory	characterized by	promissory, satisfactory
ose	full of, like	grandiose, verbose, morose, bellicose
osis	state of, disease	hypnosis, neurosis
ous	filled with	amorous, nervous
ry	quality, condition	ribaldry, thievery
tion	state or result of	disputation, condition
tude	quality of	plenitude, lassitude
ty	state of	quality, humility
ure	result of, condition, organization	verdure, exposure, nature, pressure, tenure, legislature

Catalog

If you are interested in a list of fine Paperback
books, covering a wide range of subjects
and interests, send your name and address,
requesting your free catalog, to:

McGraw-Hill Paperbacks
1221 Avenue of Americas
New York, N.Y. 10020